The Cat Rules

Also by William J. Thomas

Never Hitchhike on the Road Less Travelled

The Dog Rules (Damn Near Everything!)

Margaret and Me

Malcolm and Me

Guys—Not Real Bright and Damn Proud of It

Hey! Is That Guy Dead or Is He the Skip?

The Tabloid Zone: Dancing with the Four-Armed Man

The Cat Rules

(Everything, Including the Dog!)

William J. Thomas

VIKING
CANADA

VIKING CANADA

Published by the Penguin Group

Penguin Group (Canada), 90 Eglinton Avenue East, Suite 700, Toronto, Ontario, Canada M4P 2Y3
(a division of Pearson Canada Inc.)

Penguin Group (USA) Inc., 375 Hudson Street, New York, New York 10014, U.S.A.
Penguin Books Ltd, 80 Strand, London WC2R 0RL, England
Penguin Ireland, 25 St Stephen's Green, Dublin 2, Ireland (a division of Penguin Books Ltd)
Penguin Group (Australia), 250 Camberwell Road, Camberwell, Victoria 3124, Australia
(a division of Pearson Australia Group Pty Ltd)
Penguin Books India Pvt Ltd, 11 Community Centre, Panchsheel Park, New Delhi – 110 017, India
Penguin Group (NZ), cnr Airborne and Rosedale Roads, Albany, Auckland 1310, New Zealand
(a division of Pearson New Zealand Ltd)
Penguin Books (South Africa) (Pty) Ltd, 24 Sturdee Avenue, Rosebank, Johannesburg 2196,
South Africa

Penguin Books Ltd, Registered Offices: 80 Strand, London WC2R 0RL, England

First published 2006

1 2 3 4 5 6 7 8 9 10   (RRD)

Copyright © William J. Thomas, 2006

Manufactured in the U.S.A.

ISBN-10: 0-670-06623-0
ISBN-13: 978-0-670-06623-0

Library and Archives Canada Cataloguing in Publication data available upon request

Visit the Penguin Group (Canada) website at **www.penguin.ca**

Special and corporate bulk purchase rates available; please see
www.penguin.ca/corporatesales or call 1-800-810-3104, ext. 477 or 474

In memory of my sister Joan
and her "handsome boy," Dustin

CONTENTS

THE PET RULE

Some men are born to cats, others have cats thrust upon them.

GILBERT MILLSTEIN, FORMER JOURNALIST, *NEW YORK TIMES*

There is one rule that all pet lovers know instinctively and by heart.

Like most pets, it's also short: *NO MORE PETS!*

From the moment we bring a pet into the home, we know how this adoption act will end—in all likelihood, we will end up burying our little bundle of affection and fur. We never say this aloud, of course, but we know in our hearts that it's true. Biology dictates that we will outlive our pets. Unfortunately, this does nothing to soften the blow or ease the grief when the inevitable happens.

At the time, we comfort ourselves with clichés—"It was for the best," "It was time," "He had a great life," or "I did everything I could for her." But that doesn't change the fact that they have up and died on us, which is eminently unfair.

I am dead against scientists researching ways to prolong my life. While I don't want to live longer, I do want to live *better,* which is why I want those scientists to come up with modern medical miracles that will allow my pets to live as long as I do—and perhaps just a little longer. Let the damn dog stand over my grave and cry his fool head off for a change! See how he likes it, eh?

So we spoil them rotten and love them too much and sleep twisted up like a pretzel so as not to disturb them in bed, and they still die on us. And when they do, we recite the rule: *NO MORE PETS!* It's the one rule that trumps all other pet rules. As if it's part of some weird divorce ritual, we say it three times and turn our backs on all replacement offers.

Way back when I lost my little Malcolm—the cat that swaggered like John Wayne and ate like John Goodman—I was devastated.

"But, Bill," they said, "eighteen years is pretty good for a cat."

No, I wanted Malcolm for eighty-eight years. I wanted him to do that trick where he stands on his hind legs and growls like a sick dog, and I wanted him to do that trick … at my wake.

NO MORE PETS! I repeated softly as I carefully put the red mahogany urn with his ashes in a place of honour on my fireplace mantel.

Numb, I finished *Malcolm and Me: Life in the Litter Box,* the book I had started writing about his life. As I dropped the manuscript into the "Out of Town" slot in the big red mailbox in front of the Port Colborne Post Office, I whispered: *NO MORE PETS!*

And this time I meant it: *NO MORE PETS!* Unfortunately, as every true pet lover knows, that rule has a shelf life of only three months.

THE TOP TEN PET RULES

That Are Also Big Fat Lies

RULE 1
No more pets! Period. And this time I mean it!

RULE 2
Okay, but just for the night. In the morning, he's gone.

RULE 3
Just a couple more days and I'll find her a good home. I promise.

RULE 4
If worse comes to worst, we can always
take him to the Humane Society.

RULE 5
I did put the poster up at the store;
somebody must have swiped it.

RULE 6
I don't know where he is. He probably heard
you bad-mouthing him and took off.

RULE 7
I did not. She must have snuck into my bed after I was asleep.

RULE 8
I'll feed him and scoop his poop and
walk him and everything. I promise.

RULE 9
We'd better tell them Mikey flushed the fish down
the toilet; otherwise, that cat is a goner.

RULE 10
I'm not going to look. You look. Okay, then,
he's a she until further notice.

Three Months Later ...

Cats are intended to teach us that not everything in nature has a purpose.
GARRISON KEILLOR, SATIRIST, HUMORIST, AND AUTHOR

I have, for twenty years, written a weekly syndicated humour column that appears in forty small- to medium-sized newspapers across Canada. The readers of my column, many of whom send me notes and clippings and stuff, are some of the most thoughtful people in the country.

When Malcolm passed away, people sent me sympathy cards, poems, photos of their own dearly departed. One sweet lady sent me an embroidered and framed portrait of him. Another bought him his own tree, tree #489, to be exact, in the Crawford Lake Conservation Area, just outside of Campbellville, Ontario.

How ironic—in life, he couldn't climb a tree; in death, he now owns one.

Yet another woman made a "substantial" donation in his name to the Ontario Veterinary College in Guelph. I have since tried to have this money re-routed through a numbered company in the Cayman Islands and into my personal account at my local credit union, but no, these people have rules.

However, a few of the readers of my column are as bad at listening as fenceposts are at hearing.

After I put Malcolm to bed for good, I wrote a painful column announcing the death of my long-time companion. (Long-time companion? Well, although Malcolm was male, same-sex, different-species marriage was never seriously considered.) I ended his obituary with the pet lover's mournful mantra: *NO MORE PETS!* It was right there at the bottom of the page in caps and bold type. I even put the exclamation mark in caps.

This, however, did not stop Carole Hallpike of Caledonia, Ontario, from sending me a letter about the most gorgeous young cat in the world—a cat, she insisted, that I absolutely, positively needed to have as my own. A stone carving of a large human ear went out to Mrs. Hallpike—the award for Worst Listener of the Year. Her letter was so pathetically sentimental and grotesque in its gushiness that the mailman who delivered it was played by a soap star from *Days of Our Lives*.

Ably carrying on the tradition of, as she put it, "a long line of batty English," Mrs. Hallpike began her letter innocently enough, with an expression of sympathy for my beloved Malcolm and a description of her own personal menagerie: chickens, assorted farm animals, two house cats, one unicorn, several wildebeest that had actually appeared in crowd scenes on *Mutual of Omaha's Wild Kingdom,* and a stranger. Her husband. No, sorry. Her husband was a professor at McMaster University and spent a lot of time in Hamilton, but she still recognized him when he did come home. The stranger was a stray cat. But not just any cat.

On page two of her letter, Mrs. Hallpike cleverly developed the character of this loner, "a six-month-old male tabby with short hair and a white shirt-front and paws to match." In a description that reached near-biblical proportions, she told me about his coat of many colours—brown, black, and beige, with strains of orange. He was mysterious but charming, handsome but somewhat aloof and cool—*very* cool. Like Gary Cooper, he was the strong, silent type; a feline of few words. Her letter was like a treatment for a man/cat buddy road film, and I was immediately able to both empathize with this cat and imagine him playing opposite Johnny Depp, in the role of the Gypsy who abandoned him.

On page three, Mrs. Hallpike detailed the unfortunate circumstances that saw this poor waif left alone in the bleak countryside by people she could only imagine to be so vile and so insensitive that even today they were probably sending money to the Committee to

Reincarnate Brian Mulroney. At this point, Mrs. Hallpike was very close to plagiarizing the "babe in the manger" story. Or worse, committing copyright infringement on Tennessee Ernie Ford's song "Big Bad John":

Every morning at the barn, you could see him arrive.
He stood 1 foot 1, weighed 13 pounds and ready.
Kind of broad at the shoulders, narrow at the hips,
And all the animals knew you didn't give no lip …
… to Teddy?!?

Page four described in graphic detail the sounds, smells, clutter, and below-freezing temperatures of the barn in which she was forced to keep this "beautiful and affectionate fellow" (so that her house cats would not tear him from limb to white shirt-front). Sure enough, it was the "babe in the barn" story—with no room at the inn.

Page five—I am not making this up—started with a hand-drawn sketch of this tiger-striped orphan and ended with very clear directions on how to get to the Hallpike farm.

On page six, Mrs. Hallpike described the highly unusual but no less heart-rending scene where this poor little bastard—and I mean this in the nicest possible way—came trudging up her driveway on a bitterly cold night with nothing more than a sad look on his face and a copy of Malcolm's obituary in his mouth. Apparently, he was applying for the job.

By the bottom of page six, Mrs. Hallpike had all but emptied her cliché cupboard of phrases like "thin as a rake," "cute as a button," and "smart as a whip," but I really couldn't read a lot of it because my tears had smudged the ink and the letter now looked like the water-colour painting of the Easter Bunny that my three-year-old niece gave me for my birthday.

Can you tell me exactly, Mrs. Hallpike, which word in NO MORE PETS you had the most difficulty with? Are you by any chance dyslexic? Perhaps that particular phrase—NO MORE PETS— looked to you like MORE PETS NOW. (Please, Mrs. Hallpike, at least attend a meet-and-greet of your local chapter of DAM— Mothers Against Dyslexia!)

I know what you're asking yourself: Did he or did he not take the cat? Is he a man of his word or a wimp? Did he abide by the NO MORE PETS rule? Well, Mrs. Hallpike may not have been much of a listener, but she could sell taffy apples to denture wearers. Not only did I adopt the cat, but I started taking my mother out to lunch more often. I increased my donations to the local food bank. I quit sending old light bulbs back to the Ontario Handicapped Association for free replacements. If there had been a page seven to the letter, I'd probably be writing this column from church, in the presence of a very, very surprised priest.

Self-rationalization is one of my strong suits. I told myself I was merely going to help Mrs. Hallpike find this cat a home. I would get him out of her barn and keep him at my place until I could run an ad and find him a new owner. I was merely playing the role of an adoption agent. Yes, the great lie as told by all pet lovers—HE'S NOT STAYING! HONEST!

So I get in my little Honda Civic and drive out Highway #3, through Dunnville and Cayuga, cutting up to Caledonia along the banks of the Grand River.

When I get to the farm, they have the cat in an open box, and he's just sitting there, like an angel. He doesn't even try to jump out—he just sits there and stares at me. "So you're my next victim," he seems to say as he makes his first, best, and possibly last good impression on me. That's how very fiendish twisted cats can be. Once any other animal sets out to capture another, it chases after its prey. Not the other way around. But cats somehow manage to trick *you* into pursuing *them*, and trapping yourself in the process.

The older of the two Hallpike kids tells me that the cat just wandered up to the barn one day and started playing in the hay. I wait for him to deliver the next line, which I'm sure will be something like: "Then he drank from the cow and jumped clean over the sow." I start looking around for a hidden camera, thinking this might be some sort of *Hee Haw* setup. At this point, I decide they for sure have named him Big John.

But no, they had named him Teddy, which I thought was a great name ... for a stuffed bear.

"And then, once this big mean dog came into our backyard"— the girl was talking now—"and Teddy climbed up the tree. And then, when I called him he jumped right into my arms, and we all ran into the barn while the dog was still barking up the tree!"

Great, I thought, I'm not just getting a cat. I'm getting the plot for a Disney movie—*Teddy Outsmarts 101 Dalmatians*.

This cat calmly staring up at us from his box had, in a very short time, become a mythical character in the rural landscape of Caledonia.

Then Mrs. Hallpike recounted that every time she got down on all fours to weed the garden, the cat would jump up on her back and remain there until she had to stand up.

"He fell asleep like that one day," she said. "He's such a beautiful and affectionate little fellow." With that, I realized she was way overselling this cat. I mean, once the sucker—sorry, the client— has agreed to buy the car, you don't take him back out to the lot to kick the tires again.

"Well," I said, "I guess me and Teddy here better be on our way." God, I was hoping the kids wouldn't start crying, but at the same time, I couldn't bear another legendary tale about how Teddy saved the children from a band of rabid skunks by harnessing up the horse and buggy and evacuating everybody to Binbrook.

"Bye-bye, Teddy," they yelled as I picked up the box and put it on the front seat of my car.

"Thank you," said Mrs. Hallpike. "You won't be sorry."

Hell, I was already sorry. I just hoped Teddy didn't get me into some sort of high adventure that involved a car chase and ended with road spikes.

I started to close the flaps of the box, but those large green eyes of innocence assured me that cardboard incarceration was absolutely unnecessary.

As I drove the fifty miles back to Wainfleet, he just sat there in his brown box, looking at the passing scenery and occasionally at me, like an angel. To be perfectly honest, he let out an ungodly shriek as we were going through Caistor Centre, but hey, doesn't everybody? Calm, cute, pleasantly uninterested in his relocation situation—Teddy appeared to have been slipped a Quaalude before I arrived.

The instant I got him home and in the house, he leaped out of the box and, before my very eyes, turned into a freaking terrorist.

He ran around the house like a miniature cougar that had been diagnosed with hemorrhoids and treated with jalapeño-pepper paste. He was one bad blur—up the chair, over the table, under the bed, down the hall, up the drapes. He looked like a different cat— the kind that performs with Siegfried and Roy, and one day decides that Roy looks an awful lot like a lamb chop.

After he'd knocked over everything in the house except the retaining wall, I got him outside in hopes of calming him down. He promptly ran down the driveway and across Lakeshore Road, where he disappeared into the dense bush and shallow swamp. And he did not return.

For two hours, I called for him along the road and over the ditch, which wasn't easy, considering he didn't yet have a real name. I then drove into town and had a handwritten poster photocopied so I could distribute it in my neighbourhood. Also not easy, since I had yet to take a photo of the little misfit. That's not to say, however, that there weren't police sketches of him still posted in and around the Caledonia area.

And when I got home from town, there he was, sitting on the step at the kitchen door and looking at me as if to ask, "Where the hell have you been?"

He also seemed a little annoyed that it took me so long to unpack Malcolm's stuff in order to feed him supper.

In the first week alone, he destroyed two screen doors by clawing and diving headlong through them when he wanted out; he knocked over and smashed a Portuguese antique serving tray shaped like a fish; and he walked out of my office with the telephone cord wrapped around his neck, cracking the receiver as it flew from the desk to the floor. And as if all that did not qualify as a crime spree, my neighbour caught him hiding inside his bird feeder, waiting for some unsuspecting and no doubt endangered species to fly in.

I'm not pointing fingers, but unfortunately, Mrs. Hallpike, your "beautiful and affectionate little fellow" has ties to the Syrian-backed Hezbollah.

I can't tell you how much I looked forward to Christmas—the tree, the strings, the bells and balls, and a cat that was a demolition expert in another life.

Truth be known, as psychotic as Teddy turned out to be, the batty Caledonia matchmaker actually saved me from a fate worse than death. I mean, that was a close call. If Mrs. Hallpike hadn't pawned the little bastard (technically) onto me, I would have been forced to spend that Christmas with *people*. Thank you, Mrs. Hallpike. I said THANK YOU! (I tell you, she's the worst listener in the world.)

"Teddy! Get off the ceiling, buddy. That's where spiders sit."

CATTITUDE

Yeah, as if we care what you think of us.

THE CAT RULES

As They Apply to the Telephone

Last fall, Faith, a four-year-old Rottweiler in Richland, Washington, saved her owner's life by dialling 911 and barking for an ambulance. Faith had been trained to knock the phone off its cradle and press her nose to an emergency speed-dial button. (Strangely enough, my roommate in college used the same system to order a pizza after a long night at the Walper Hotel.) Fortunately, cats do not use the telephone, or yours would be calling the Humane Society every time dinner was late. But if cats did use the telephone, we'd need some rules.

RULE 1
Only one cat can use the phone at one time.
Party lines are a thing of the past.

RULE 2
No, that's not what a "catcall" means.
Don't use obscenities and you'll be fine.

RULE 3
The cat's calls are restricted to family members and local friends.
No commercial calls whatsoever.

RULE 4
Yes, technically in cat years you are a teenager,
but four hours on the phone every evening is still too long.

RULE 5
No, you can come in the house and use the phone
in the kitchen, like I have to do. Sorry, no cellphone.

RULE 6
The number of the fish shop has been blocked. Don't even try it.

RULE 7
Quit phoning the dog next door and hissing into the receiver.
He's probably got catcall display.

RULE 8
The bill is $2,010. You dialled Tokyo and then fell asleep, stupid.

RULE 9
You call Miss Mew one more time
and they'll charge you with stalking.

RULE 10
If you phone the vet and cancel your annual checkup
one more time, I'll get the thermometer and do it myself.

Cats and Dogs—*Vive la Différence*

Women and cats will do as they please,
and men and dogs should relax and get used to the idea.
ROBERT A. HEINLEIN, AUTHOR

In celebrating the uniqueness of cats and dogs, people often resort to the phrase *"vive la différence,"* which is French poodle for "I don't care if I look ridiculous with this haircut; I am from Fronnnce."

I dearly love both cats and dogs, and I do not like the simplistic polarization of cat lovers versus dog lovers. This is yet one more divisive split between once moderate and tolerant pet owners that I also blame on President George W. Bush.

Although I deeply appreciate both cats and dogs, I also adore their differences. In fact, I toyed with the idea of calling this book *Dogs Are from Mars and Cats Are from under the Couch.*

A dog is like your best buddy. He's right there beside you, come hell or high water. A cat is also like your best friend—*until* it comes to hell or high water. Then you're walking through the valley of death all alone, because somebody has to stay by the phone in case you call home for help, and besides, it's pretty much time for my nap. "You go get 'em, killer," the cat will say. "I'll be here when you get back."

It has been said that a friend will help you move, but a real friend will help you move a body. A dog is a real friend. A dog would indeed help you move a body. "I'll pull on his shirt, Bill, and you lift his feet." A cat is also a real friend, in the sense that he will call 911 and keep them posted on your progress. But give you a hand? "I'm a cat. I weigh thirteen pounds. I can't lift no stiff."

A dog is like the stupid brother-in-law you never had. A cat is like the clever lawyer you never want to have staring at you from across the courtroom.

A dog is a go-along, get-along kind of guy. A cat is like a female accountant—she wants all the details before anybody makes an official move of any kind. Plus there are the mood swings to contend with.

When something isn't right with your dog, he'll let you know by throwing up on the new rug. When something is not right with your cat, she'll demand a full review of your relationship. And then she'll also throw up on the new rug, just one inch from the hardwood floor, where it would have been a breeze to clean up.

When a dog meets another dog, the two will sniff each other from head to bum and then usually take turns peeing in the same spot for the remainder of the day. It's not unlike a meet-and-greet at the Waverly Hotel.

When a cat meets another cat, there follows so much screaming, hissing, and caterwauling that you think you're watching an episode of *The Osbournes* where Ozzy and Sharon suddenly sober up and realize they're married to each other.

Dogs almost always get an A for friendliness towards other mutts. Cats never receive a report card marked, "Gets along very well with his playmates."

When a dog meets a houseguest, he gets so excited that it's all he can do not to pee his pants—and he's not even wearing pants. Bring the toy, give the paw, nose the crotch.… Okay, a little too friendly, perhaps.

When a cat meets a houseguest, he sizes that person up like a cynical customs officer. How long are you staying? Any goods or contraband on your person? Been around any stupid dogs lately? How'd you like a little fur on your pant legs? And if that person is smart and a cat lover, he will step away from the cat's advances, say he really doesn't like cats (or better yet, he's allergic to them), and then go sit down on the couch. Presto! The cat is in his lap.

Dogs go only where they're wanted; cats love to go where they're not.

Dogs like to wear clothes. In winter, dogs like to wear dog sweaters. They'd prefer baggy sweatshirts with "I'm Just Here for the

Beer" written on the back, but they'll settle for a nice tartan wrap.

Have you ever tried to put a sweater on a cat? It's a safe bet that before you can get the cat to accept clothes, you'll be wearing a straitjacket yourself. Cats come into this world naked, and they're going out wearing nothing more than a disapproving smirk.

Ignore a dog and you hurt his feelings. Ignore a cat and you're just granting his fondest wish. "When it's time for the buddy-buddy, rah-rah nonsense, Bill, I'll get it started, okay? In the meantime, ignoring me is respecting my space."

Raise your voice to a dog and he'll slump to the floor with a bruised ego. Raise your voice to a cat and he'll glare at you for so long and in such a way that you'll find yourself voluntarily enrolling in an anger-management course.

A cat can also save you a lot of time and effort. Give a dog an order and he wags his tail and wiggles his bum and smiles, and you think, I have a shot here. I could train this animal. Give a cat an order and the cat gives you the finger. End of the training session right there. Guys understand the finger. They get that a lot. And with all the time you've saved, both of you can now take a nap.

CATTITUDE

Raining cats and dogs:
Absolutely the weirdest effect yet of global warming.

THE CAT RULES

As They Apply to the Dog

Fighting like cats and dogs is not just a saying.
In some households, it's a way of life.

RULE 1
Family cats and dogs should try to get along like children.
Okay, children who are wearing electronic ankle bracelets
and are under twenty-four-hour surveillance.

RULE 2
Cats and dogs should cohabit in such a … Look, I don't
care who hit whom first. If I miss the end of this game,
you're both going to live in the tool shed.

RULE 3
No, two dishes are for two animals. They're not
the appetizer and entrée of the complete dog dinner.

RULE 4
I told you, you don't have to do something
to deserve it. She's a cat!

RULE 5
For the last time, that dog is not your pet pony to ride around
the kitchen. Stop it. He's developing a facial twitch.

RULE 6
I think her point was that if your nose was where it was
supposed to be, it wouldn't be bleeding right now.

RULE 7
Go ahead, let her clean your face.
Just keep your eyes open and stay alert.

RULE 8
Stop it! Both of you! Or I swear I'll turn this car
around and nobody will go to the pet show.

RULE 9
So the dog gets the main floor and I gotta stay
in the basement? That's pet apartheid.

RULE 10
Okay, so she's taken over your doghouse.
I'm still not taking you to the Cathouse for Dogs.

Teddy Got His Bum Stuck
and Came Out Weggie

I called my cat William because no shorter name fits the dignity of his character.
Poor old man, he has fits now, so I call him Fitz-William.

JOSH BILLINGS, AUTHOR AND HUMORIST

At the start of week two, Teddy was walking leisurely around what was left of the house, surveying his new digs like the lord of the Sunset Manor. (Apparently, even superheroes take a day off once in a while.)

He gave the corduroy couch a few bounces. Cool. He turned up his nose, down in the basement. Too cool. He walked across the kitchen counter and got his bum slapped. Not so cool. He took a nap at the foot of my bed, in a spot that catches the noonday sun. Warm. He perked up his ears every time a wave rolled over the sand beach beyond the lawn. Odd. He inspected his freshly filled litter box. Acceptable, but not preferable to the great outdoors. He rode the rocking chair in the TV room like a drugstore cowboy. Very cool. He screamed at the kitchen door to get out and got a lecture about running wild through the neighbourhood like a deranged stray with a history of violence. No, you're not in rural Caledonia any more, Teddy.

And for most of the day, he carried on inspecting the premises, which, begrudgingly, met with his approval. The obvious absence of farm animals and fresh hay didn't seem to bother him all that much.

However, at 5:55 p.m., when I was gearing up for my TV news hour, I heard this ungodly screech from the living room.

In a panic, I rushed into the room to find him … not there. Did I actually hear that unearthly scream, or had my neighbour cranked up Céline Dion again? I was peering up the chute of the fireplace when he did it again from behind the couch. I peeked over the back of the sofa, and there he was with a toy mouse in his mouth. He was stuck in the corner where the couch met the baseboard radiator. Apparently, he found one of Malcolm's toys back there, and when he turned to jump back out, he got his bum wedged under the rad and the rest of himself pinned to the wall by the back of the couch. As I would come to learn, Teddy was, for those few fleeting moments, as well behaved as he would ever be. I took this opportunity to laugh like hell, what with him momentarily immobilized and unable to retaliate. I should have taken a photo. That's when I heard, for the first time, a low, ominous growl come out of his mouth.

I pulled the couch forward, and out sprang the cat formerly known as Teddy with the mouse in his mouth and a new, more appropriate name: Weggie. The farmboy super-cat that could leap tall trees in a single bound got his arrogant little ass caught in the vise-like grip of the ever-villainous baseboard radiator. The Disney plot thickened.

Once freed, Weggie quickly forgot the embarrassing gaffe and began relentlessly battering the mouse around the room until he whacked it back under the couch, exactly where it had been in the first place. He then walked away nonchalantly, as if nothing had ever happened. He went into the bedroom, jumped up on the bed, found his sunny spot, and stretched out for a long, well-deserved nap. The learning curve on the stranger in my house was arcing fast, and I was spinning in my sneakers to catch up.

CATTITUDE

Nervous as a cat in a room full of rocking chairs:
Or, in a kennel full of dogs in heat.

THE CAT RULES

As They Apply to Naming Your Pet

RULE 1
If you name your cat Kitty, I will personally come
to your house and see to it that you are bitten
on the bum by a dog named Blackie.

RULE 2
Try to find an original name. Morris, Garfield, and the Cat
in the Hat have been taken. No, Fido is not original or funny.

RULE 3
For a sister/brother duo, Misery and Company work for me.

RULE 4
Catastrophic is taken. I'm saving it as a backup for Weggie.

RULE 5
Okay, but he's gotta be really bad to be called Saddam.

RULE 6
Top, Fraidy, Copy, and Pussy are all poor choices. Missy, Muffin, Patches, Punkin, Muffy, Fluffy, and Buffy are even worse.

RULE 7
Try to tie a trait to the name. For example, a motherly cat would be Teresa, promiscuous Slick Willy, gaseous Rush, and larcenous Martha.

RULE 8
No Nuts is rude, and my cat Malcolm hated that nickname as much as he did the operation itself.

RULE 9
Humorous names by breed can work. The Balinese Falcon, the Birman of Alcatraz, and the Persian Gulf are all good.

RULE 10
Also, the Sweater Twins might work. ("He's Persian, eh? And his sister's name is Angora.")

4

Matching Pets with Proper Owners

A dog is like a liberal. He wants to please everybody.
A cat doesn't need to know that everybody loves him.

WILLIAM KUNSTLER, RENOWNED CIVIL RIGHTS LAWYER

The first order of business in adopting a pet is compatibility. It is always preferable to seek out a pet that looks up to you as a friend, not down on you as food.

"Excuse me, Siegfried, how about insisting that Roy's next pet is a puppy, okay?"

There's a book out there titled *Know Yourself through Your Cat*, which devotes an entire chapter to choosing your cat by colour and coat pattern. I am not making this up.

Imagine—with millions of perfectly good cats and dogs wasting away in animal shelters, we are publishing guides that recommend adopting designer cats that match the drapes.

The jest … sorry, the gist of this theory is that you can interpret your own personality through the colours of the cat you choose to adopt. For example, if you choose a ginger-coloured cat, it's because his masculinity, directness, and self-will reflect your own vitality, energy, and independence. A black cat symbolizes the feminine mystique and speaks to your inner beauty and spiritualism.

Right. And a white cat means you like vanilla ice cream and look good playing tennis, while a blue cat acts as a warning to keep the food dye (and the cat) away from the kids.

Trying hard to know myself through my cat, I took a long look at Weggie. There I saw a loner—a mutt in a mishmash of coloured stripes, taking life day by day with no real plan in place—and it revealed to me the aging humorist, destined to die a bitter alcoholic, alone on a treeless island.... Okay, fuggeddaboutit. We scrapped that idea. Self-awareness is not for everybody, okay?

More recently—and you had to know science would stick its nose into the pet-selection process—veterinarians at Cornell University in New York state have developed personality tests for kittens and puppies to help potential owners select animals that are sure to suit their personality and lifestyle. The vet I heard interviewed on the radio revealed that the purpose of the study was "to avoid a sourpuss pet."

Although he did not mention Weggie by name, I still took exception to this kind of mudslinging being directed towards my cat. I also wondered if the name Sourpuss was already taken.

Obviously, the vets at Cornell got their testing ass-backwards. If you test the kittens and puppies, you will get a good read on the suitability of the pet. But in all relationships, the more intelligent of the two partners is the one most capable of adapting, of compromising, of making it work. Therefore, you must test the person so that the pet can succesfully analyze the owner before he takes control of the relationship.

For instance, you should not be testing to find a quiet, withdrawn puppy to go with an introverted person. Go the other way. Look for a guy who likes to drink water out of the toilet. Then you've got a potential owner who has something in common with every dog on earth. Suddenly, the possibilities for harmonious couplings are endless.

Don't be testing a puppy for a bubbly personality. Find a woman who loves to chase a stick into the icy waters of a lake and bring it back in her teeth, and the world's Labrador retrievers will beat a path to her door.

Learn that trick where you balance the biscuit on your forehead, wait for the command, then flip it into your mouth, and there won't be a dog within fifty miles of your house that doesn't want to be your best friend.

Find a man who eats the hot dog and leaves the roll, a man who whines uncomfortably while watching nature programs on television, a man who can jump seven feet into the air and land with a Frisbee in his mouth—there isn't a canine alive that wouldn't want to warm the foot of his bed and bring him his slippers every morning for the rest of his life.

You show me a guy who scratches himself with his feet, and I'll show you a dog that will cry real tears when left at the door in the morning.

Analyze the person, and the pet selection becomes simple.

Although with cats, it gets a little trickier. Generally speaking, if you pretend to dislike everything—including them—they'll love you till death do you part. Hence, for perfect feline matchups, you need people who can act.

For instance, if you are willing to pretend you don't like cats, and will even fake sneezing fits when you get near them, word gets around. Pretty soon, like reformed drunks direct from an AA meeting, cats will begin showing up at your door at all hours, trying desperately to win you over.

Before you know it, you and your chosen pet will be rolling around on the floor like two bad kids at summer camp. If you look closely, you'll notice that the cat has a stupid grin on his face. That's because he knows he's just been named Salesman of the Month.

Those are the male cats. Female cats don't gloat. They just bat their eyes, roll over on their backs, and leave you wondering exactly who conned whom.

If you're a woman who can nap while everything around you dissolves into chaos, or who can nonchalantly clean your eyebrows with spit from your hands during a home invasion, you will find cats taking a number at your back door to rub up against your leg.

Show me a man who can reap two hours of entertainment out of a ball of string, and I'll sell you a one-way ticket to Kittyville.

You want to give a cat the gift of a lifetime? Buy one of those expensive wood-framed, padded cat boxes, as advertised in *PETS Magazine*. Leave the price tag on it. Place it in the cat's favourite spot. After three days, remove it, untouched. Then accidentally leave an empty box from the liquor store in the kitchen. This box will weaken and collapse from overuse, about an hour before the cat does. Later, exchange the expensive box for food. It's called good home economics.

You can sit in the den with a blanket on your lap and call your cat to come and cuddle until you lose your voice. That little beggar ain't budging. Why? Because you want him to.

Order the cat to stay put while you go off to a quiet corner of the house and pretend to read a book. Presto—cat on the lap, head between the pages.

Ideally, you want to select a feline that will not attempt to murder you with his claws when you put him in soapy water. A cat that will actually enjoy taking a bath. Yeah, well, I'd like to be shipwrecked with Sandra Bullock on the island of Porto Santo, okay? Some things are just not meant to be.

Let's move on.

Pet personality tests are revealing but ultimately useless. It's obvious to me that after 113 years of American veterinary science, the doctors are still buying the big lie. It doesn't take a framed degree on your wall and jars full of tapeworms in your fridge to know that the real owner in the people/pet relationship is the pet.

So in almost every selection situation, any cat or dog will do just fine—that is, as soon as the pet appraises you and then barfs on the results. This officially establishes the true authority of the household.

One more time: you/can-opener person + the prince or princess of petdom = relationship.

The adoption equation: you/subservient can-opener person + the dominant prince or princess of petdom = bumpy but enormously satisfying relationship.

If you do not catch on to the program right away, don't worry about it. Pets know that good training takes time. They'll be patient; they're not going anywhere.

CATTITUDE

Sweeten the kitty: To up the ante.
Literally. Kitties could not be sweeter.

THE CAT RULES

As They Apply to Mismatched People and Pets

RULE 1
Never adopt a pet that outweighs you.

RULE 2
Adopting a dog is like taking in a pet. Adopting a cat is like opening a boutique hotel called Chez Moi.

RULE 3
Always select the runt of the litter. He tries harder.

RULE 4
Never adopt a white cat after Labour Day.

RULE 5
When possible, adopt two pets of different ages—like Princes William and Harry, the heir and the spare.

RULE 6
Never adopt a pet that comes with a muzzle,
a mug shot, and a cease-and-desist order.

RULE 7
Never adopt a pet based on looks alone.
Remember, you were once cute too.

RULE 8
In a choice between a pedigreed pet and an animal
of undetermined origin, always go with
"Eenie, meenie, minie, mutt."

RULE 9
If you can ride it around the backyard, it's not a pet.

RULE 10
If the pet can ride you around the backyard,
you are one sick puppy.

5

The Purr Heard Round the Room

To err is human, to purr, feline.
ROBERT BYRNE, AUTHOR AND HUMORIST

For long periods of time, Weggie is a very quiet cat. That is, until he needs something. Then he vocalizes in such a way that dogs two counties away put their paws over their ears and run for the best-insulated room in the house.

Quiet I love, so I was quite pleased to have taken in a roommate who maintains silence around the house. The waves splashing softly on the beach beyond the breakwall, a breeze rippling gently through the leaves of the huge lakeside maple tree, the muffled motor of the hummingbird darting back and forth at the feeder just outside the kitchen window—these were sounds both Weggie and I stopped to appreciate, to savour with a cock of the head but not tarnish with a comment.

I liked my new silent partner.

One day, a Friday, I had shut down the shop, and I came into the house to try out a low corduroy couch and two matching chairs I had impulsively bought while passing by a sidewalk sale on Toronto's Yonge Street. The couch and one seat were chocolate brown; the other was beige. They were belted so you could tighten them up when they began to lose their shape.

The pieces had arrived that morning, and the delivery guy was kind enough to help me carry them into the house and put them in place—the couch on the wall opposite the fireplace and the chairs to the right and left of it. I tipped him with the old furniture.

I almost tipped him with my cat.

"Does he go with the furniture?" he asked as we both looked into a deep cardboard box to find Weggie playing imaginary war games at the bottom of it. The box was in the driveway, behind the truck.

I just stared at him, trying to imagine how he could have possibly got into a box that was as tall as my armpits. He must have first leaped onto the tailgate of the truck and then dived straight down into the box.

When I didn't reply, the driver repeated his question: "Frisky, there? Is he part of the deal?"

In my best Jack Benny, I put a hand to my face and said, "I'm thinking. I'm thinking."

So now it was the end of the day and the beginning of a weekend, and I placed a glass of red wine on the leather-bound table I'd hauled back from Barcelona in the late seventies. The tabletop showed an old map of the world, and drinks were most conveniently placed mid-Atlantic, just over the Azores.

I bobbed around in both chairs, tightening one belt and loosening the other. Then I propped myself up on the couch with throw pillows to make sure I could see both the fire and Morgan's Point off in the distance but still reach my drink. Perfect.

Of course, when a person is perfectly comfortable, it's a signal to a cat to somehow interrupt regular programming with a bulletin that says, "Hey! It's me! Pay attention!"

Weggie jumped from somewhere I couldn't see, straight into my lap, forcing me to move my wine quickly out of harm's way, to a spot just south of the Canaries.

And he looked every bit as surprised as I was that he had flung himself into my lap.

Until then, we had been getting more comfortable with each other quite gradually. Weggie had finally begun sitting beside me, at arm's length, on the pullout couch in the TV room. This was a big step. Occasionally, I'd reach over and pat his head or scratch his back, and he would reciprocate with a look that said, "Is that really necessary?"

Now, as he stood on my lap, I thought maybe he'd mistaken me for an empty cardboard box.

We were staring at each other rather warily, and for quite some time, when suddenly Weggie gulped as if he had swallowed something. Then, from somewhere back where his nasal passage meets his throat, he emitted a very odd noise.

It was just one "thhrrrit," short and quick, and it was over almost immediately. It sounded like a toy airplane trying to start up before three or four tugs on the cord finally get the engine going.

He swallowed hard again, and once more the noise erupted— "thhrrrit"—scaring him a bit and puzzling me a lot. I was sure something was stuck in his throat.

Somewhere around the fifth "thhrrrit," Weggie's little motor caught fire, and to the utter amazement of us both, he started to purr. I began to laugh loudly, which only added to the discomfort he felt in producing some strange, vibrating murmur he'd obviously never made before.

Soon, he began to knead, yet another mannerism I'd never seen him display. Now, I've had a cat knead in my lap before, and if everything is perfectly misplaced, it can be the most painful experience a man will ever know, short of falling asleep drunk in Lorena Bobbitt's bed.

The only time this happened, it was rather noteworthy because, although the cat was safely thrown clear, I clung to the ceiling for several minutes with my fingernails dug into the tiles.

So I clipped Weggie gently behind the hind legs a few times, and he sprawled out and rolled over on his back, which, as any woman who sleeps with a snorer knows, causes the purring to become twice as loud. The only thing more intense than his sonorous breathing was my non-stop laughter.

I stared at him, shaking my head and scratching his belly, and wondering what ever happened to Tough Guy Teddy.

Absolutely vulnerable, he just lay there purring, with four paws kneading the air and the smallest trace of drool glistening at the side of his mouth.

Although thoroughly embarrassed by the thought, I couldn't help feeling like a giddy man hearing his child say his first word.

Except, of course, that this was weird and unexpected, and I could feel his body vibrating as the thrumming went into overdrive. He seemed to be sleeping, except for the occasional gulp of air that jolted his eyes wide open.

I was touched by the fact that this cat, now two years of age, had not until this moment in his life felt comfortable enough with me to purr.

On my new couch on a Friday in the fall of 1994, my cat and I had finally bonded. On a cloud of throaty humming, there rose between us a trust that would never be broken. I loved the little bugger, and in some weird way that guys connect but are too creeped out to talk about, he felt the same way.

Purrfect. I loved my new, not-so-silent partner. If he took to swigging red wine, I'd have to high-five him.

CATTITUDE

*Purrometer: A scale for measuring
how well a cat likes his dinner.*

THE CAT RULES

As They Apply to Vocalization

RULE 1
No purring after eleven o'clock at night. It's a cat curfew.

RULE 2
It's not a game. Besides, you can't purr louder
than the TV; I've got the remote.

RULE 3
Good Lord, come up for air once in a while.
Are you drawing air from the back end?

RULE 4
You keep purring in overdrive, and eventually you'll wear it out.

RULE 5
When you purr in the middle of the night,
you wake me up. Then I dream I'm mowing the lawn.

RULE 6
You're ruining every sweatshirt I own.
Try purring without drooling.

RULE 7
Your new name is Placido José Luciano,
for one of the Three Tremors.

RULE 8
I can't control his barking. And no, it's not the same thing.

RULE 9
I know it's stupid. But wagging his tail is his way of purring.

RULE 10
Just once in a while, couldn't you be in a bad mood and sulk?

6

All Things Bright and Beautiful
Are Joining the Revolution

No tame animal has lost less of its native dignity
or maintained more of its ancient reserve.
The domestic cat might rebel tomorrow.

WILLIAM CONWAY

News reports of dogs and cats committing violent acts against their owners used to be rare, but today we seem to be suffering through an epidemic of pet-on-human horror stories.

Believe me, when that farmer's German shepherd in rural Alberta shot him in the ass a few years ago, it was the news highlight of my week. It seems the man had left his rifle on the ground while he worked in the garden near the house. The dog began to roll around on it, to try to scratch his itchy back. Jumping to his feet, he accidentally hit the trigger, shooting his owner in the rear end.

When the man passed out, the dog pulled him by his shirt and trousers around to the front of the house, where he was spotted by a passerby, who called an ambulance.

Authorities were at a loss as to what to do about the shooting and the subsequent rescue. I thought the dog should serve thirty days in a minimum-security kennel and, while there, receive the Order of Canada in a ceremony attended by several hundred local dogs barking, "We're not worthy."

This was an assault with a deadly weapon that had a happy ending. But recent news reports have been full of astounding examples of animals in full-blown rebellion mode.

In New Zealand, a couple of rams in heat took exception when interrupted by a couple bent on ruining their fun. The stampede ended with a shutout: Rams 2, People 0.

In Australia, a huge white whale off the coast of New South Wales—perhaps tired of watching his species be decimated—took a run at two guys fishing in a fifteen-foot boat and sent them flying into the sea. Experts believe the whale was just cranky. Nobody was killed, so we'll just file this one under "The Attack of Moody Dick."

In Alexandria, Egypt, a man named Waheeb Hamaudah had tethered a sacrificial sheep to the roof of the three-storey building where he lived. He was fattening the animal up for an upcoming religious festival.

Believing that all sheep go quietly to the slaughter, Waheeb was casually checking on his fleecy captive one morning when, all of a sudden, "Head butt!" Breaking the silence of the lambs in spectacular fashion, this woolly soldier of the animal revolution sent his would-be slayer sailing off the roof and into the street.

Waheeb Hamaudah was fifty-six. He had been preparing the sheep for Eid al-Adha, the Muslim feast of sacrifice.

The revolt of earth's mistreated mammals is now officially underfoot ... sorry, under way.

Just as Waheeb took flight over Alexandria, a pig named Charlotte tried to hijack a U.S. Airways plane heading from Philadelphia to Seattle. The pig was flying first class, which—and I want to stress this emphatically—is no reflection on the well-to-do of Philadelphia.

Maria Andrews, the owner of Charlotte, claimed that the three-hundred-pound pig was her best friend. Again, I must emphasize that this has no bearing whatsoever on how hard it might be to establish relationships in the City of Brotherly Love.

Producing a doctor's note that characterized the pig as a "therapeutic companion pet" similar to a guide dog, Maria won the porker the right to travel in the cabin instead of in the cargo hold.

At first, nobody objected to Charlotte's presence (except, of course, those who had ordered the pork shoulder sandwich for lunch). By all accounts, she behaved quite well, sleeping for most of the flight. But then the plane prepared for landing and the hog went wild, squealing and charging around the cabin, discharging feces as she went.

Near the end of the tirade, Charlotte tried to break into the cockpit, presumably to take control of the aircraft and fly it to a country where they refuse to eat meat on the hoof.

Somewhere in this madness, James Herriot—perhaps the kindest vet domesticated animals ever had—was attacked through the hedge of his farm in southern England by a neighbour's flock of angry sheep. A broken leg for the man who wrote *The Good Lord Made Them All*—this was the cruellest cut of all.

The first wave of the war against man's inhumanity begins in the wild and in the sea, but it spreads quickly—from farms to domestic air flights to the middle of your own living room.

Last night after supper, I stretched out on the couch with Weggie burrowed deep into a blanket on my lap and flicked through the channels to the Public Broadcasting System.

"Tonight on *Nova*," boomed the clipped British voice of the narrator, "we visit, high above the arid desert of East Africa, a towering mountain chain with a bizarre climate."

Weggie dug in deeper and covered his ears with his paws. He'd killed his limit earlier in the day and really needed a nap.

"It's hard to believe any animals could live here," bellowed the narrator, "but these endangered species live *only* here—marooned on a mountain island in a sea of clouds."

Weggie sat up. Itsy-bitsy endangered animals? Trapped where they can't get away?

"Africa—as you have never seen it before! Journey to Kilimanjaro!"

Weggie had no idea where Kilimanjaro was, but he sure liked the sound of it.

Both of us looked on with mild curiosity as the sacred Kilimanjaro community paraded across the screen: elephants, zebras, mountain sheep, water buffaloes, wildebeests, and highland rock hyraxes, which look like Canadian beavers that have been to a really good orthodontist.

I chuckled when a rampaging elephant burst into a secluded glen and interrupted two lions mating. Weggie gave me a dirty look, not unlike the one the male lion gave the elephant.

For most of the show, Weggie didn't show much emotion, but when a rare East African bongo antelope began falling behind the pack and limping badly, he started to lick his lips. I know this sounds silly, but I'm kind of proud of the fact that Weggie's a bit of an overachiever.

So he was displaying the normal and calm demeanour of any Canadian household pet that watches one to three hours of educational television each day. That is, until the slender-billed, chestnut-winged starling, which mates for life, began screaming with delight while bathing in a mountain stream.

Weggie went ballistic.

Off the lap, over the arm of the couch, and onto a shelf in front of the TV he leapt, bashing at the screen with his front paws while standing erect on his hind legs.

The starlings floated to the bank of the stream, and Weggie went with them, beating on them all the way. They soared to their nest in the rocks next to a waterfall, and Weggie banged on the screen even harder when he heard the cheep, cheep, cheeping of the chicks.

Oblivious to the danger lurking in my TV room, this rare pair of starlings flew off into a dazzling forest above the clouds around Kilimanjaro, and Weggie jumped through my rack of home videos, around the back of the set, to see if they came out the other end.

If there's one thing both of us learned from this program, it's that the nearly extinct and very elusive slender-billed, chestnut-winged starling has survived to this point mainly by confining its movements to its own safe habitat—that is, inside the TV set.

The evening of interactive TV programming continued with Weggie hiding behind a pillow when the Mackinder's eagle owl began circling lazily over a stream. At the very sound of the word "bird-mouse," he began to salivate, this combination being, on a good day for Weggie, both entrée and dessert. Yet he backed right off when the long-legged, spotted serval cat killed and ate one of the few remaining members of the striped mouse family. This may simply have been an act of professional courtesy.

Who could ever have foreseen the day when some of the worst violence in the world comes from watching nature programs with your cat? Who knew that one day we'd need a channel blocker to prevent our pets from watching public broadcasting? Do we now require warning ribbons at the bottom of the TV screen: "Viewers are advised that the following program contains scenes that may cause your pet to go completely berserk, making him think, at least temporarily, that he is George, George, George of the Jungle"? The mere sight of the rare Kilimanjaro crested rat, helpless on a limb of a tree, sent Weggie's bum wiggling, and he was just about to dive headlong through the screen of my sixteen-inch Toshiba when I changed the channel.

Weggie was disappointed but relieved that it was all over. He curled up in my lap, and we both fell asleep watching *NYPD Blue*.

That's it. PBS can keep its educational programming in the can for all I care. For my cat, it's strictly the Mighty Morphin Power Rangers and the Road Runner from now on.

I urge you to take a good look at your pets. Sure, they're the sweetest things since Christmas cake, but make no mistake about it—they're just a few genes removed from a pack of wild dingoes or a pair of cougars, and they have no respect whatsoever for your vaunted position on the food chain.

All creatures great and small are mad as hell, and they're not going to take it any more.

The message couldn't be clearer if it came written with letters clipped from a newspaper: be kinder and gentler to all the beasts, or be prepared for a furred world war. (Sorry. I watch too much TV.)

Remember, you heard it here first.

CATTITUDE

Cat-o'-nine-tails: A lucky charm; one tail for every life.

THE CAT RULES

As They Apply to Domesticated and Wild Animals

RULE 1
If it purrs, let it be; if it roars, set it free.

RULE 2
If your husband likes to entertain guests by sticking
his head in the cat's mouth, it's not a pet.

RULE 3
If your cat sleeps beside you in bed, it's a pet.

RULE 4
If your cat sleeps in the bed and there's
no room for you, put locks on the doors.

RULE 5
If your cat is a finicky eater, it's a pet.

RULE 6
If your cat is consuming forty pounds of freshly
killed meat a day, do not run out of food.

RULE 7
If your cat receives free samples of new
pet food products in the mail, it's a pet.

RULE 8
If your cat receives royalties from *Mutual of Omaha's Wild
Kingdom* in the mail, get yourself a cage and never leave it.

RULE 9
If the cat is running your household, it's a pet; if the cat
is ruining your house by jumping through rings
of fire, contact Barnum & Bailey.

RULE 10
No, I will not change your name to Che.
And yes, everybody's ass looks big in camouflage.

Weggie and the Screen Door

It is easier to hold quicksilver between your finger
and thumb than to keep a cat who means to escape.

ANDREW LANG, POET AND NOVELIST

Weggie has just been inducted into that exclusive club of brainiacs known as Mensa. Normally, this elitist organization of intelligentsia only accepts people with the highest IQs in the world, but they've made an exception in my cat's case. (I understand Lassie had all the votes necessary for acceptance, but then that idiot Timmy got his foot stuck in a railroad tie and Lassie had to go and save his sorry ass for the umpteenth time, causing him to miss the Mensa interview.)

Anyway, Weggie was recognized because he was able to prove that he is approximately three to four times smarter than his new owner. That would be me, the guy who oversees the three-hundred-dollar screen-door budget.

You see, when Weggie wants to go out, he views the screen door between him and the great outdoors as about a ten-minute tunnelling job. I know this because, although I have not actually seen him do it, I have replaced four screens that had cat-size holes in the bottom right-hand corner. It's either Weggie or I have ants that escaped from Stephen King's last novel. Four screen doors destroyed and the summer's barely begun.

Four perfectly good screen doors chewed and clawed clean through at the rate of one every two weeks. In my house, a bag of potato chips lasts longer than a screen door. The only good news is that Weggie can't wield a hammer; otherwise, there wouldn't be a window left in this house.

Now you may think I'm exaggerating, but if you drive through the town of Port Colborne, you'll notice that Reichman Lumber on Main Street is offering a "Weggie Special." Basically, the deal is that if your cat goes through a screen door four times, the fifth repair job is free. I am not making this up.

It's just fortunate that Weggie is less than two years old, and therefore is protected by the Young Cat Offenders Act—otherwise, I'd have disciplined the little bugger … sorry, burglar, by now.

The other day, I was coming up from the lake when I heard him biting and digging through mesh again, trying to get out. I grabbed from near the door a bucket of water that I use to rinse beach sand off my feet and threw it at the screen. By the time I got into the kitchen, there he was, dry as a bone and sitting calmly at the edge of this little lake on the floor, drinking from it. What could I do? You can't whack a guy for having a drink. (If you could, my name would be Welt, not William.) Besides, Weggie's teeth are a bright white these days—I think the mesh has a flossing effect on them.

Yet another time, in the middle of the night, I heard the snapping of wire mesh and crept into the kitchen with a rolled-up newspaper in hand. Right there, under the cover of darkness, I smacked the cowering little culprit two or maybe three times. Yes, standing naked while still mostly asleep, I gave my rubber boots the thrashing of their lives. No sir, they won't try to escape in the night ever again. Meanwhile, back in the bedroom, Weggie was circling a spot at the foot of the bed, just settling in for a good sleep. Did I mention that he's smart and really, really fast?

I was returning from a neighbour's cottage one evening when I heard the unmistakable sound of teeth and claws on wire, on … let me see, I believe it was screen door number three. I keep track of the doors I have had rescreened by the humiliation factor that comes with taking them to be repaired.

First one, Frank at Reichman Lumber said: "Whatta you got, like a circus cat or something? This is the strongest mesh we sell!"

Second one, Frank and his staff said in unison: "Oh, not again."

Third one, Frank said: "Forget it. I'm puttin' in sheet metal this time."

Fourth one, Frank said: "You know, most guys wouldn't replace this screen. Most guys would replace the cat."

So when I heard the gnashing of metal mesh, I crept to within ten yards of the kitchen door and grabbed one of the rubber boots I'd previously beaten half to death. Holding it just over my right shoulder in the quick-toss position, I crouched behind a shrub and waited for the little monster to snap one more strand of wire. And I waited, patiently, because this was the shot that was going to be heard around the neighbourhood. I was going to throw the boot with all my might at the water pail, and the splashing, I was certain, would be enough to deter any further tunnelling through screen doors.

And I waited, in this frozen live-action pose, because I knew when that boot hit the bucket in front of his face, Weggie would never touch another sliding door as long as I let him live. And I waited, in this coiled and ready-to-lunge position, until my lower back went numb and my throwing arm fell asleep.

I stayed so long in that contorted posture that I wasn't sure if I *could* resume a normal stance, or ever straighten up again.

And when I moved my neck to the left, to ease the pain in my shoulders, I saw him. You see, the house makes an L shape around the kitchen patio, and there he was in the living-room window, staring at me. He had been sitting in that window for the entire twenty minutes I had been standing like a statue of a man holding a rubber boot (minus the pigeon poop). It's a good thing I was so sore, or I might have hurt myself laughing.

After we had stared at each other for one additional minute—with me unable to unfreeze my stance without suffering serious muscle damage—he looked past me towards the road, hoping to catch just a glimpse of that turnip truck I fell off on the way into town.

Then he looked back at me, and I swear he shook his head. It was a "way too much TV, Bill" shake of that arrogant but very handsome head. Then he licked himself and went to bed. I went and soaked in a hot tub for an hour to regain the feeling in my back and upper body.

Did I mention he's a really smart little fella? But I'll catch him vandalizing that screen door. You can count on that. Of course, when I do, about the only thing I'll be able to do is push my walker in his general direction to scare him a little bit—but I'll catch him, of that much I am sure.

CATTITUDE

Cat burglar: A nimble crook who normally breaks into, not out of, the house, stupid.

THE CAT RULES

As They Apply to Going Outside

*No destructive behaviour in the home will be tolerated by the cat,
and discipline must be administered if such inexcusable conduct persists.*

RULE 1
A really good way to exit any building is to sit and meow
at the door. This has worked exceedingly well for most cats.

RULE 2
Nothing is that important on the other side of the door.
No, frog season goes on for the whole summer.

RULE 3
"When you gotta go, you gotta go" applies to peeing
or pooping. That's why we have a litter box.

RULE 4
No, I can't leave the door open.
Murray the Cop knows where my beer fridge is.

RULE 5
You like punching holes through metal?
Try this—it's your dinner in a tin can.

RULE 6
"Not a big deal"? You don't have to face
those guys at the lumberyard.

RULE 7
No, there's not a chance in hell they're laughing *with* me.

RULE 8
You were not doing the prep work for a cat flap. You're lying.

RULE 9
One more time and I'm going to show
all the other cats your neuter scar.

RULE 10
I'm serious. If I need to get a fifth screen door,
you're going through it without the hole.

8

I Want My Cat's
Health Care Program

Really, what are veterinarians but doctors without hospitals and summer homes on Lake Joseph? Vet clinics are sanitary and cheap, and the employees give you treats if you behave. There are no lineups, no forms to fill out, no beds in the halls. There's no glassed-in room down the corridor where a couple of old German shepherds in housecoats are smoking their brains out. Plus, if you have to stay overnight, there's always a friendly pet around to keep you company. I want my cat's health care program. It's twice as good as mine.

This idea came to me the other day as I sat in Dr. David Thorne's veterinary clinic on Clarence Street in Port Colborne. I was coughing all over the list of errands I had to run while I was in town. The words "Boggio's Pharmacy—cough medicine" were top of the list.

The vet clinic was not crowded; the receptionist was not bitchy; and I didn't have to fill out fifty-six forms in white, yellow, and pink triplicate. I thought to myself, This place is so unlike a real hospital that it really ought to be one.

Now, our leaders keep telling us that the health care system in this country is in grave danger because it's simply too expensive to maintain at the current rate. Yet we have three to four times as many veterinary clinics as hospitals. As far as I can see, the vet clinics are clean, well run, and unsubsidized by government—and they have a much better selection of magazines.

Call me crazy and have me admitted, but isn't the answer to create a new satellite system of small medical centres where you will be able to kill time in the waiting room playing with your pet? A pet-friendly people hospital where your health card covers medical treatment for both you and your Jack Russell?

To be fair, of course, your local hospital will thereafter have to admit household pets for heart transplants and the occasional de-fleaing. But generally speaking, pets are a lot better behaved in the waiting room than people are anyway.

Think of the savings. An overnight stay in a hospital costs four hundred dollars. At the vet's, you can board your dog for fifteen bucks a night. Cats stay for ten dollars, and children under twelve accompanied by an adult cat can stay and eat free. (Sorry, that's the teaser for the Family Weekend Getaway Special that Dr. Thorne and I are working on.)

The average person entering a hospital for surgery stays three to four days. That's $1,200 to $1,600 on the health card tab. The average person having surgery in a vet clinic is going to leave as soon as he wakes up beside a drooling Saint Bernard that has just had a major tooth extraction. Even if the boarding fee for a person is $25 a day, the government will save $1,075 to $1,475. And just think—you get to ride home in one of those neat little wicker travelling cases. No, this is a great idea.

Okay, so we extend the holding cages a few feet, install a telephone and CD player, and provide free breath mints for any pet you have to be with overnight. But we'll still be saving loads of money and easing the pressure on our currently overloaded health care system.

How many times have you been in a semi-private hospital room with a fellow patient who is moaning and groaning and keeping you from watching your favourite soap opera? What happens? The nurse runs in, lifts his gown, and gives him a shot of Imovane. Not only has that sedative just cost $63.79 in tax dollars, but you've also been mooned in the process.

This can't happen at the vet's.

If you create a disturbance in a vet clinic, the assistant runs in, opens the door to your cage, and raps you on the nose with a rolled-up newspaper. Cost to government? Nothing. Look on your face on the take-home video? Priceless.

There will be absolutely no mooning at these new satellite clinics. Not only will you be provided with a gown that has a front (and this idea alone deserves front-page treatment in the *New England Journal of Medicine*) AND A BACK—but all pet patients will be required to wear them as well. And no entertainment fee will be charged when you try to get a cat into one of those medical gowns.

Television rentals in hospitals cost about ten dollars a day. When you get bored at the vet's, they just throw a ball of wool in the corner and let two kittens loose.

Vet clinics provide fresh kibble for dogs and high-protein meat dishes for cats. At one time or another, we've all eaten hospital food, right? Okay, so we come out dead even on that one.

I know what you're thinking. You're thinking, Oh sure, Bill, vet medicine is fine for the small stuff, like wart removal, ringworm, and declawing mean sisters who scratch their little brothers in a fight over the remote. But what about major, complicated surgery?

Are you kidding? Medical experts are already cloning pigs to grow organs for future human transplant operations. But you won't find pigs roaming around your local general hospital now, will you? Pigs belong in animal hospitals. You go to the animal hospital for a transplant and it's one-stop shopping! Plus, you get your pick of the litter.

There's just one rule, and I want every veterinarian and veterinarian's assistant across Canada to understand it, memorize it, post it over the examination table, and tattoo it on their forearms. To determine the body temperature of a human patient, the thermometer goes in under the tongue, okay? Absolutely no exceptions!

CATTITUDE

The cat that got the cream: Like the early bird
that got the worm—only with more calories.

THE CAT RULES

As They Apply to Health Care

RULE 1
Getting a cat into his cage for the trip to the vet's
only looks like animal abuse. It's for his own good.

RULE 2
Remind the cat that the carrying case can be short-term
transportation or long-term incarceration. It's his call.

RULE 3
Stay off to the side while holding the cat down on the examination
table. Missiles can and will be launched from both ends.

RULE 4
Trust your vet and ignore the patient when he says,
"He feels me up all the time, Bill; the guy's just weird."

RULE 5
Humour your vet with responses like,
"Sure, I'll brush his teeth. Start first thing in the morning."

RULE 6
For headaches and dizziness brought on by the cat's
psychotic destruction of the house, dissolve two
Tylenol tablets in warm milk. Failing that, lock the cat
in the basement and head right for the Scotch.

RULE 7
When administering a pill to a cat,
always wear steel-reinforced welder's gloves.

RULE 8
Pill-proof goggles are also a good idea.

RULE 9
Save time and blood—pretend that pill is a suppository.

RULE 10
When the vet informs you about bad breath,
frequent urination, and persistent wheezing, leave
immediately. He's in no shape to examine your cat.

9

Weggie—A Work in Progress

Cats are like Baptists. You know they raise hell, you just can't catch 'em at it.
JIM STAFFORD, SINGER/SONGWRITER

So what exactly is a Weggie? My Weggie is a lovable but clever little creep who, if human, would be doing community service by now as part of a way-too-lenient probation agreement. Hey, I'm kidding, of course. Knowing Weggie as well as I do, I'm sure he'd pay two dumb cats to do his community service while he went off on a hunting expedition at an exotic rodent ranch.

Not that Weggie looks like a criminal. He's a very handsome cat with perfect tabby markings, green eyes, and white fluffy fur on the underside. Surrounded by rust-coloured fur, his pink nose has a black dot birthmark on its very tip. Not to boast, and with all due respect to your cat, my cat is the most handsome cat in the whole wide world. Is too! Is too! Is too!

And he's fit. Finally fully grown, this cat is long and lean and can leap backyard fences in a single bound. I've never seen a faster cat. His speed afoot and dexterity of paws are remarkable. Weggie can pick off a sponge ball in mid-air and come down with it still clasped in his paws. I swear that if he could turn a double play and switch hit, I'd need a sharp stick to keep the Blue Jays brass at bay.

Weggie will be three this Christmas, and he's lived in my house for all but the first eight months. Thanks to Dr. David Thorne's scalpel, Weggie skipped the sexual maturation stage of cat development that behaviourists call the "juvenile period" and became a gelded young offender straightaway.

Just a little advice here: once the dastardly deed is done, deny, deny, deny.

"I have no idea what you're talking about."

"I took you in for a routine check-up. They must have gotten the charts mixed up."

"A boxer, eh? Well, that certainly was his lucky day."

"Absolutely not. I will not ask the vet to prescribe Viagra."

Weggie has the darting eyes of a poker player and the quick gait of a thief. He can sit perfectly still for an hour, if that's what it takes to ambush a bird. He can crawl so slowly and so low to the ground that a rodent only inches from the nest is a certain snack. It would not surprise me in the least if someday I discover a cache of tiny burglar tools and a deck of credit cards belonging to wealthy but naïve victims.

Weggie, however, is not defiant. For the most part, he abides by my house rules, if only as a way of humouring me. In this, he's exceptional. For instance, he never walks across the stove and along the kitchen counter any more … except when I'm not there. He never kneads his claws into the leather chair in the living room any more … except when I'm not home. He never crosses the road any more … except by following a different route each time. ("But, Bill," my neighbour John says, shaking his head in wonder, "he always looks both ways before he crosses. I've watched him do it!") And he always comes in from outside when I call him … except when he'd rather not.

Yes, if Weggie gets any more exceptional, I'm going to present him with a blue ribbon of achievement and put it on very, very tightly.

Catch him doing something wrong and he's the picture of nonchalance: "Oh boy, I haven't scratched this spot in weeks. What's that? Me? Do that? Do you really think that if I'd done something that bad, I could sit here and lick myself in this totally disinterested manner?"

When all this too-cool-for-conviction stuff fails, Weggie simply pretends to be distressed by some invisible thing off in the distance, which entirely distracts me until I investigate and find it's something that's actually … invisible.

Weggie's so-called recreational behaviour is very well developed. He can gallop, roll, jump, climb, and fight imaginary opponents through the bottom rungs of chairs with the best of them.

On the other hand, his ability to hide silently behind a door and attack my ankles as I walk by with something resembling dinner on a platter may be overdeveloped.

Then there's the game of "stick."

Weggie strolls with me along the beach for a fifteen- or twenty-minute walk. He runs in the sand at incoming waves and then backpedals the minute they break and threaten to soak him.

I walk as he climbs onto concrete breakwalls, jumping from one rampart to another, making sure I'm watching his athletic antics. He's up on a lawn, then down to the sand, examining dead fish and hiding behind hedges.

As long as there are no dogs around, he'll go as far down the beach as I do.

But there's one spot I cannot walk by without playing stick. It's an old cement breakwall with the name "Racey" painted across the front in white letters. It's run down, with weeds and hedges growing here and there, and an old set of weathered wood steps going from the top of the wall to the lawn.

I can't remember how this started, but whenever we pass this breakwall, I pick up a stick and run along the sand, crouching low so Weggie can't see me from the top of the breakwall. He then engages in a fiercely fast attack-and-retreat manoeuvre that absolutely kills me.

He jumps out of the weeds, slaps the stick a couple times, and then hides behind the steps. I run the stick a few more feet along the edge of the wall, and he bursts out from behind the steps, bats the hell out of the stick, and dives back into the weeds. The stick moves, he bolts—wham, bam—and scurries up a small tree in retreat.

This goes on until I can't take it any more.

Not a man easily brought to laughter, I'm kept in stitches most of the time by the antics of this cat. I always quiet down before a normal person hears me cackling and calls the cops, though, because with Weggie up a tree, I know I would appear to be alone.

Then I start running for home, and Weggie scurries close to the beach to chase me.

When he catches up, I stop dead, and he stops dead. Then he makes this really weird move, prancing sideways towards me with all four legs stiff. It's the damnedest thing. With a mischievous expression on his face, he stalks me by dancing laterally towards me, and it's all I can do to keep from buckling at the knees, laughing.

Then it's a foot race to the house—with me sprinting down the shoreline and Weggie scampering under cottages and over porches. And I know, no matter how fast I run, that cat will be sitting at the kitchen door waiting for me when I stumble breathlessly onto the patio.

It's our thing, the stick-and-race-ya-home game.

There's also our daily whack-and-smack game. While pretending to be asleep, Weggie will give me a gentle shot with his paw as I walk by the foot of the bed. On the way back out of the bedroom, I'll gently give him a shot in return. Then he gives me another shot and I give him one back, and then his nails come out on the next exchange and I give him a swat for being too rough. So he bites me and I pick up a big book, and the next thing I see is a guy in a striped shirt skating into the bedroom blowing his whistle. He physically separates us before I can "shirt" the little roughneck, whose fur is standing on end.

Oh no, Weggie can play all right, which is why I've spared no expense on his Christmas gift—a form-fitting Rottweiler costume that comes with a scary barking device I can activate by slapping my right ear with my right paw.

Man, how things have changed around my ... er, his ... um, *our* house. It seemed at first that Weggie had a heart colder than an actuary's, but now he's beginning to warm up to the idea that it's just him and me. It helps that I have the tools to open cat food cans.

Really, the last thing we guys need is an outpouring of affection. Once that door has been opened, it's just a vicious cycle of crying jags and self-help groups, with getaway weekends to try to find our inner selves.

And that's why I'm so taken by this cat—he's really just a guy in fur.

And that's also why I think I made a great choice in selecting his name. Because if he wore clothes, that's exactly what I'd like to do—run up behind him, yank his shorts straight up, and give the little waif a wedgie.

In fact, when I put on the Rottweiler costume on Christmas Eve, I might just do exactly that. Merry Christmas, Weggie, you little rapscallion. Oh, please stop the purring. I'm starting to tear up. (Did I mention he's as cute as Garfield was before he gained all that weight?)

CATTITUDE

Purranoia: The irrational fear that although your cat appears happy and content, he's actually plotting your demise.

THE CAT RULES

As They Apply to Play

RULE 1
Fully extended claws and completely bared
fangs are signs that playtime is over.

RULE 2
You hiss at me once more and I'll get the water pistol.

RULE 3
Don't you dare spray. It is not the same thing as the water pistol.

RULE 4
More catnip? The neighbours already
think we're running a grow-op.

RULE 5
So what if the cat next door has a carpeted play station?
If he runs up the telephone pole and onto the power
lines, are you going to follow him?

RULE 6

You got yourself up there; you get yourself down.
No, the fire department said next time they'd bill us.

RULE 7

Okay, so the ball tied to the doorknob is a stupid game. Let's tie it
to the car bumper of that lady who delivers our mail instead.

RULE 8

No, I will *not* get you another canary. That was cruel.

RULE 9

No sneak attacks. What are you, Javanese?

RULE 10

It's called "fetch." Dogs love this game.
Now can I rest for a while? Please?

10

Animal Dating—It's a Jungle Out There, Jim

Prowling his own quiet backyard or asleep by the fire,
he is still only a whisker away from the wilds.

JEAN BURDEN, POET AND AUTHOR

Recently, the pet world has been the focus of some amazing technological advancements. One such breakthrough—sidewalks that flush—is my own dog invention, I'm sad to report. Think about it! You could walk the streets of Paris again and look up once in a while.

We have created almost as many gadgets and gimmicks for our pets as we have for ourselves. From dog collars with emeralds and flashing lights to a parrot cage with running water to pet daycare centres that rival the Four Seasons for luxury, we have spoiled the little ones rotten.

I spent a summer as a lifeguard at the Long Beach Conservation Park on Lake Erie, sleeping in a tent that was not nearly as comfortable as Tuff's Softcrate, which has pockets, fresh air flaps, and comes in four sizes.

Believe it or not, there is now even a computer bank, called the International Species Information System (ISIS), that acts as a matchmaking service for zoo animals.

Shocked? I know what you're thinking. It's not fair. The last time *you* had a date, you went to see *Midnight Cowboy* and were stunned by the resemblance between Ratso Rizzo and the guy your minister fixed you up with.

And now Nikki, the Toronto Zoo's stump-horned rhino, has a choice of four mates, all from exotic countries, and all blessed with horrid bad breath (which stump-horned rhinos adore). It's *The Bachelor* with bad bodies.

Of the 200,000 zoo animals already registered on ISIS, there are 761 mammals, of which more than 100 are lonely chimpanzees. The operator of the ISIS system says the most pressing problem he has had to deal with so far is keeping the home addresses and phone numbers of those eligible chimpanzees away from Michael Jackson. (Bubbles is reported to be so jealous that he's refusing to wear the little military uniform that matches the one Michael has.)

Seriously, ISIS not only lists vital statistics on the prospective mates, but also provides detailed information about the animal's ancestors to enhance the possibilities for reproduction.

Somehow I can't see this ancestral information working for human dating services. "Yes, honey, after we're married, we'll be spending a lot of time with my relatives out in New Brunswick, shown here in our annual family reunion photo. What? Well, yes, it does appear that my great-aunt Lilly forgot to put clothes on that day, and no, I don't know why she's bent over with her back to the camera, but as you can tell by the visor she's wearing, it was an unseasonably warm winter's day."

I don't mean to make light of this dating system for animals. Frankly, there's probably nobody in the whole world hornier than the albino wildebeest in downtown Sydney that peeked at the computer one day and now knows there's a real fox ... sorry, a really beautiful, sole-surviving female albino wildebeest named Betty sleeping restlessly in Seattle.

It's just a little surprising to discover that the first truly successful newlyweds on the information superhighway are two sweaty anthropoids that are more than willing to do it right there on the shoulder of the road.

And you have to be very careful. We've all heard of the unfortunate mixups that have been made by dating services for people.

Like that divorced truck driver from Melville, Saskatchewan, who was so desperate for a wife that he paid more than five thousand dollars to a Toronto dating service to help him find wedded bliss.

Unfortunately, because of a computer glitch, they matched him up with a bilingual bricklayer from Buckingham, Quebec, who was also seeking a wife.

And while that particular relationship is, in fact, working out—mainly because of their shared love of fishing and unfiltered Players—you have to be extremely careful when dealing with endangered species.

Press one wrong button on the ISIS computer network, and into the conjugal cage you've put a giant-jowled Indian rhino with a fur-bearing Malaysian tapir.

And of course, we all know what you get from the mating of these two rare species—an exceedingly dirty look from the tapir!

What with viruses and mischievous kids with home computers, all kinds of mixups could occur now that ISIS is in place. Let's say you are a warm, attractive SWF, 36, who enjoys afternoon naps, long walks, campfires, the circus, and sweets. You're searching for Mr. Right, someone who shares all these favourite things, and the dating service puts you in touch with Ben, your perfect match.

Oh sure, he may well enjoy all those things, and he may even show up at your door with a box of chocolates and doing a little stutter step to amuse you. But don't be fooled—Russian black bears are easily trained to behave that way. Bring a muzzle along on that date, just in case—as my mother used to say—he tries something funny.

Because when it comes to dating, as *Wild Kingdom*'s Marlin Perkins used to say—while safely locked inside a Jeep, watching his assistant, Jim, be physically and sexually assaulted by an enraged female Bengal tiger in heat—"It's a jungle out there, Jim."

CATTITUDE

Meow Mix: A meet-and-greet hosted by a feline dating service.

THE CAT RULES

As They Apply to a Bad Date

RULE 1
Never let your cat date a dog.
These inter-species relationships never work out.

RULE 2
Never let your cat date a tom that claims he's looking
for love and a family but has already been neutered.

RULE 3
Lay down the law early: "Just say no to catnip."

RULE 4
Make sure your cat takes her own bottle
of milk—date rape drugs are everywhere.

RULE 5
No matter how late or how far, she can always
call you to come and pick her up.

RULE 6
Okay, so her date has tattoos and earrings.
Has he been dewormed?

RULE 7
I don't care if all the other cats are sleeping over. You'll stick to
your curfew or be grounded, which means no tree climbing.

RULE 8
Why can't you just order an anchovy pizza
and spend time with him in the rec room?

RULE 9
Be home by midnight or your cat flap will be locked.

RULE 10
I want to speak to his parents.
No, the dog chaperone is not good enough.

Weggie—A Twice-Convicted Cat Burglar

*The cat, of course, never breaks a rule. If it does not follow precedent,
that simply means it has created a new rule and it is up to you to learn it quickly.*

SIDNEY DENHAM, WRITER

Normally, I'm in a pretty good mood when I wake up in the morning. Normally, a gentle paw to my nose puts a smile on my face, and my eyes open onto the mischievous face of Weggie sitting up straight and staring at me, quite prepared to give me another wake-up shot if he has to.

But one morning was different. After he clocked me in the nose, Weggie bounded out of bed and ran into the living room. As I rose up on my elbows to follow his hasty retreat, I noticed the crime scene at the end of the bed.

It was not a normal day, or a laughing matter.

That day, I discovered that a serious breach of privacy—indeed a criminal act—may have been committed right in my own home, right there at the foot of the bed. The proof was in the torn manila envelope, the pieces of tinfoil, and the crumbs.

You know, you live with somebody for years and think you know him, and one day you wake up to find him dazed and demonic-looking, hiding behind a door and holding a soapstone carving of a loon…. Oh, sorry, that's what happens when you're Aline Chrétien and you wake up at 24 Sussex Drive with two weirdos in your bedroom (one of whom is your husband).

Anyway, it appeared that I had become the victim of mail fraud in my own home. That's right, mail fraud—by male feline. Just the thought of a stranger running his filthy hands all over my personal belongings made me feel violated; I felt as if my face had been licked by a large inside worker with postage-glue breath.

I had received in the mail a package clearly addressed to me, with proper name, location, and postal code, etc. Having taken receipt of the package—which was filled with promotional materials and samples of a pet nutrition product—I placed the bulky envelope, hereafter referred to as Exhibit A, on my bed for the purpose of late-night perusal, after I'd read the paper and finally completed the crossword puzzle by jamming "drive" into a four-letter box for a word meaning a golf shot.

At precisely 4:34 p.m. on the day in question, I interdicted a crime pursuant to Section 8.3.10 of the Canada Post Violation Code, which states that any article of domestic post forthwith and knowingly recepticated by … At this time, I would like to introduce Detective Jack Webb, who has just entered this story without knocking or even producing a search warrant.

"Just the facts, sir. Just the facts."

Okay, that little bugger Weggie chewed off the corner of the envelope, pulled out the plastic bag of sample treats, and ate them—leaving crumbs all over the comforter at the end of the bed! And I wasn't really pleased about it.

I would have turned the little felon over to Canada Post, but they'd likely have lost him for several years in the Stoney Creek Sorting Station.

The first thing I did was call the people who sent me the pet product. I asked the first CANUSA representative available if they were manipulating the levels of organic zinc in this supplement, which could cause a mineral-deficient cat to commit such a crime. I told her what had happened. She was aghast. But she wasn't slurring her words or anything, which was good.

She said, "Let me get this straight. We sent you samples of and promotional materials for CANUSA, our new pet nutritional product; we put the correct address and postage on the envelope; and *you received it*?"

Oh boy, suddenly we had two Canada Post investigations in the works.

When Canada Post told me it was out of their hands (what a sense of humour), I phoned the police.

I explained the situation, and the officer was most accommodating. He said he'd come right over and shoot the cat. That's when I realized that I'd somehow been patched through to the Buffalo Police Department in nearby New York State. When I called the local police station to ask what the cat could be charged with, the officer on duty was much more helpful. And intuitive.

"So we're dealing with a cat burglar here," he said gruffly. "How about theft under $5,000?"

"Well," I said, "it was a pretty small sample bag. It would be more like theft of $4,998.01 under $5,000."

"You could do what a lot of people do at this point in the crime: throw in a Rolex and some diamond rings for insurance purposes," said the sergeant.

I knew two things. First, Weggie was not a jewel thief. And second, if he ever figured out the barter system—carats for cat treats—I'd have to be really quick about getting a safety deposit box at the bank.

"Ah, here we go," said the sergeant. "Private mischief."

Private mischief? It's as if they had a file on that little deviant. If Weggie's little theft ring ever expanded enough that he needed an office, that's how the nameplate on his desk would read: Weggie Thomas—Private Mischief.

"Yeah, here it is. Everyone who wilfully destroys or damages property commits mischief," quoted the sergeant.

"Let's add the leather chair with the scratches, the broken fish platter from Portugal, four screen doors, plus the case of wine he hasn't let me near for five months, and go back to that theft under $5,000 thing," I suggested.

"Either way, we can nail him. He'll do two years less a day," he said.

"What if he doesn't confess? What if he gets a lawyer?" I wondered aloud.

The desk sergeant lapsed into a fit of laughter that sounded like an asthma attack.

When he was able to speak again, he said, "If that cat gets a lawyer, it'll be you holding an empty plastic bag of treats that was clearly intended for the cat. I'm sorry, but if he legals up, you're going to jail, son."

"Maybe I'll just give him a good talking-to and send him to bed without supper," I suggested.

"Good idea," said the sergeant. "As long as the lawyer doesn't find out."

Have you noticed that when you flip through the dictionary, the words "feline" and "felon" are curiously close together?

CATTITUDE

Only the cat covers up its own mess: Good advice for politicians.

THE CAT RULES

As They Apply to the Statute of Limitations on Crime

RULE 1
In the criminal justice system, the people are represented
by two separate, yet equally important, groups:
the police, who investigate crime, and the district attorneys,
who prosecute the traditionally non-feline offenders.

RULE 2
Cats always look sneaky; you really need DNA to convict.

RULE 3
Hiding toys is not a crime unless they belong to the dog.

RULE 4
Killing a goldfish is definitely a crime.
Eating the evidence can be both incriminating and yummy.

RULE 5
Just because he plays with the yellow
crime-scene tape doesn't mean he did it.

RULE 6
Hiding out in a cardboard box for three days after the crime
is discovered probably just means he loves hiding in a box.

RULE 7
Yes, there is a feline restraining order to keep him
from coming within fifty feet of his favourite rodent.

RULE 8
Of course claws are considered a weapon.
Try boarding a plane with those things.

RULE 9
No, you have to be wide awake for the entire
eighty hours of community service.

RULE 10
When it comes to pet crime, dogs confess and cats contest.

12

Advice to New Pet Owners

*If man could be crossed with the cat, it would improve
the man, but it would deteriorate the cat.*

MARK TWAIN

Okay. You refused to listen to the people at the Humane Society six months ago when they told you that giving the kids a pet for Christmas was a really bad idea.

You also didn't heed the warning of the vet columnist who said that bringing a pet into the family during the hectic holiday season would be like giving birth at Times Square on New Year's Eve with Dick Clark doing the play-by-play.

As a result, you now have this little creature bumping into door frames, in a permanent state of shock because he cannot fathom how he went from being the most cuddled, coddled, cutest bundle of joy Santa ever delivered to his present household status, which is equivalent to that of the blue box in the corner of the kitchen.

The same children who cried when they had to go to bed without the pet on that first night now can't remember his name.

At present, you're the one doing all the chores you outlined in your introductory lecture to the kids, and you're so stressed out that the last little yellow puddle you cleaned up actually belonged to you.

I am here to help. I'm a self-taught pet expert who believes in the principle of "tough love" for pets.

Unless you, as the master of the household, train that animal to follow rules and regulations that you forcefully introduce and adhere to in the strictest manner possible, then …

Excuse me.

Sorry, Weggie was screaming at the window to come in, and when he comes in, he gets a treat for being a good boy, but since I was all out of his favourite Deli-Cat niblets, I chopped up half of the orange roughy I was going to have for dinner and then lightly sautéed it in butter, just the way he likes it, and served it up with a small glass of non-oaked Chardonnay on the side.

Where was I? Oh yeah, you gotta teach those little buggers who's boss.

Properly cared for, your pet will bring you and your family a lifetime of love and happiness, not to mention a mountain of fecal waste material.

Sure, a pet will give you more attention than your spouse and less lip than your kids, but they're still animals and are, for the most part, toilet untrainable.

Here, then, are the several steps to success and happiness from my New Pet Love Program:

First, drop them gently into lukewarm water while they're still frozen in the package and … Oh, sorry, that's the New Love Peas Program I'm working on for *Vegetarian Monthly*.

Let's start again. When you first bring a pet home, keep him inside the pet carrier until he adjusts to his surroundings. This will calm him as it teaches him that the pet carrier, under certain circumstances, can serve as a jail cell. It's your way or minimum security.

Cats are as sensitive as some people, and more sensitive than most. Immediately remove all photographs of former pets. If you have the ashes of previous pet loved ones on display, do not say things like, "If only Muffy had listened to me …"

Much like your mother-in-law, pets are curious creatures that will examine every nook and cranny of your house. They will not, however, point out cobwebs or run their fingers along the tops of doorsills. Give them full reign of the house. Trust me—with them, your liquor cabinet is safe.

If there is any question in your mind about spaying or neutering your new pet, simply stand back and look at your children, then look at your husband. Can you say "vasectomy"?

Young puppies and kittens love to eat shoes and slippers. However, some specialty shops now carry booties for pets. I advise you to buy your pets their own footwear. They'll still gnaw on your shoes, of course, but when you catch them doing it, you can sit down right in front of them and eat theirs!

Always place the cat's litter box far away from his food and water station. You wouldn't set up a table for dinner in the loo, would you?

Like some non-adventurous humans, pets are very territorial. If you can pen the area around the couch in the TV room, restricting the movement of both the pet and the man of the house, your vacuuming days are over. If your new pet likes pretzels and beer, you may not hear from either of them for days.

Rough-housing? Like wrestling on the rug and rubbing his face really hard, it could prove fatal, especially if your new pet is a goldfish.

Pet-proofing your home is absolutely vital. Unplug or cover electrical cords for puppies and kittens, keep fish bowls well away from cats, and never let the children involve the budgie in their backyard badminton tournament.

Canines and felines will want to get out of the house at least twice a day. Remember, dogs go on a leash. Cats generally prefer a Lincoln Town Car.

Cats keep themselves incredibly clean but may occasionally

require a bath. Pay a professional to do it. You can't carry enough health insurance to do this job yourself.

Should your cat be missing the litter box, it's probably just bad aim. Keep your bathroom door closed; the cat is probably modelling himself after your husband.

Middening? You don't want to know.

As cute as they are, cats are born serial killers when it comes to mice, moles, and birds. You're their accomplice. Live with it.

Spraying the furniture? Make sure the wooden parts are well sanded and match the stain to the original colour.

CATTITUDE

*Meno-paws: The point in life when a woman
kicks her husband out and gets herself a cat.*

THE CAT RULES

As They Apply to Rookie Owners

RULE 1
Of course the cat will fit right in with
your household. Just as soon as the house
is reorganized according to his standards.

RULE 2
Keep the litter box clean; otherwise, it's "Any box will do."

RULE 3
Introducing your cat to a friend's cat is like setting
up your mother-in-law on a blind date with
Saddam Hussein. Keep a garden hose handy.

RULE 4
You may call it your precious table of personal
mementoes. He knows it as "the bowling alley."

RULE 5
That *was* your favourite chair. Move on.

RULE 6
Finicky? Cats invented the hunger strike.
Foodwise, you can do better.

RULE 7
Some cats just love to eat plants. She probably didn't
know it was an imported Japanese Satsuki azalea.
What? You named her Bonsai?

RULE 8
It's called "anger transference." Even though
the vet did the surgery, he hates *you*.

RULE 9
No, referring to her as a "little bitch" just
reinforces her self-image. She is. Delight in it.

RULE 10
Sorry, but you selected a Siamese. Even other cats
refer to them as the "wackos of the fur world."

My Cat's Driving Me to Temperance

The dog's tongue is softer, the cat's voice is sweeter—
and when it comes to shedding, it's a draw.

AUTHOR UNKNOWN

While watching Weggie in his sleeping position—tail and legs sticking straight out, head at a grotesque angle with his tongue lolling out the side of his mouth—I concluded that if he were human, I'd have no choice but to call the county coroner.

The closest people come to experiencing the deep sleep of a cat is that state called *rigor mortis*.

Cats don't sleep; they temporarily pass away. And I don't dare wake Weggie up. Who wants to hear about the bright light, the long-gone grandmother, and all that *Crossing Over* nonsense?

Watching Weggie enrapt in this dreamy trance, I am reminded of the story of how the Prophet Mohammed once cut the sleeve of his shirt so as not to disturb his sleeping cat, and I think now that's the kind of tender teachings I'd like to see repeated in all the mosques and madrassas of this world.

At any given time, depending on which doors and drawers have not been properly closed, Weggie has six to eight favourite sleeping spots around the house. Madonna should sleep around so well.

In winter, when the cold keeps him indoors most days, Weggie's on the sleeping circuit almost full time. At least he was, until he fell in love with a case of Bacardi rum. (When you neuter a cat that has a strange and vivid imagination, there's no telling what kind of romances can blossom before your eyes!)

No, Weggie doesn't have a drinking problem. Cats, as you know, do not drink. They used to, of course, but that was a long time ago, around 63 AD. When the Greeks first began to ferment grapes, the earliest domesticated cats drank what their masters spilled … which was a lot. This crude, powerful wine caused cats to get very mellow and friendly. When drunk, they would come when they were called; play stupid, demeaning games like "fetch"; and wag their tails whenever their masters walked into the room.

One day, nursing a brutal hangover, a cat by the name of Socrates had this blurred but grand epiphany and screamed, "By Zeus! We're acting just like bloody dogs!"

So they quit. As often happens, Socrates, fresh out of rehab, scored a sweet role in the Broadway musical *Cats*.

Occasionally, a cat will fall off the proverbial wagon. In his book *Cat Behaviour Explained,* the pet psychologist Peter Neville documented the celebrated case of an English cat that became an alcoholic. Apparently, the cat, aptly named Slosher, had a passion for Campari and soda—I'm not making this up. After three years of Slosher's daily tippling, his owner consulted Peter the pet shrink to help end this habit in the least traumatic way.

The doctor advised Slosher's owner to wean the cat off the booze by gradually adding more and more soda into his cocktails. (It may work for cats, but I believe that's what killed Dean Martin.)

Personally, I'd have recommended he quit cold turkey. As in, "Look, stupid, quit breaking into the liquor cabinet, or you won't get any more cold turkey!"

Apparently, the owner first realized that his cat had a serious problem with alcohol when the two were watching *Born Free* on television, and Slosher staggered up to the screen and propositioned Elsa.

Okay, that part I made up. But there really are cases of cats well into their cups.

Having got into the habit of consuming the leftovers from a drip dish on the floor, the pub cat of the Cock Hotel in Fforden, Wales, became a public drunk. A vet discovered that Trixie had trouble standing because she was almost permanently pissed. After a short stint in vet rehab, during which the drip dish was placed out of reach, Trixie, the six-year-old bar cat, recovered.

Today, all the patrons of the pub ignore her because there's nothing worse than a reformed feline alcoholic trying to convert anybody who will listen.

Anyway, just before Christmas, I bought twelve bottles of wine, both whites and reds, at the Port Colborne liquor store, and Brad (I know, a little too familiar, eh?) put them into an oversized Bacardi box for me.

Once home, I put the box in the kitchen near the sliding glass door and went on to other things.

In the meantime, Weggie jumped up on the box and didn't move, except to go to his dish and his litter box, for thirty-one days straight.

He loved it. It was a bed, a scratching post, a lookout, a hideout. Over time, he flattened the cardboard divider, pushed the bottles to the outside, and made himself a home. From this slightly exalted position, Weggie ruled his world, nattering at birds, hissing at the neighbour's beagle, and ordering me to get his supper.

A couple of days after Weggie took possession of the Bacardi box, while he was briefly outside torturing something smaller than himself, I removed a tall bottle of Italian white—Soave, to be exact.

Well, you would've thought I'd spooned out the solid parts from his Chunks-o'-Chicken Delight. He could no longer get comfortable; it threw the whole suspension system of his sanctuary out of whack.

He stared at me indignantly from a sitting position beside the box until I finally put the bottle back, exactly where it had been. He promptly jumped in, curled up, and went to sleep. I dropped the top over him and went to bed. Sober.

Soon, he began running to the box whenever I yelled at him for doing something wrong. It was as if he thought it gave him some kind of diplomatic immunity.

Once in a while, he would flip up the top and look into the dark recess of the cardboard box just to make sure the answer to life was still in there.

You've heard of *The Cat in the Hat*? Weggie officially became *The Boy on the Box*.

Meanwhile, with Weggie ensconced in his cardboard Shangri-La, several nearly extinct species of furry little critters were busy replenishing their stock outdoors. Soon, hundreds of mice, moles, and rats were crawling through the neighbourhood, carrying lighted candles and chanting, "Señor Bacardi has been berry, berry good to us!"

I didn't dare touch the box for fear of sending his warped little world spinning out of control.

I was so frustrated that I thought I might have to attend a meeting. "Hi, my name's Bill, and I haven't had a drink for thirty-one days."

Weggie, with his weird ways, was almost the only cat in history to drive a guy past drink and straight into abstinence. My cat had become my own liquor control board. If he dressed in a little sailor suit with tap-dancing shoes, he'd be singing, "Away with the rum, by gum, by gum."

I mean, I'm well aware that in this day and age, a man's home is no longer his castle, but when I left the liquor store, I was pretty sure that case of wine was mine.

CATTITUDE

The cat's cheers are the mouse's tears:
An emotional ride on the food chain.

THE CAT RULES

As They Apply to Alcohol

RULE 1
Never give a cat alcohol. Hell, he's already
getting most of your salmon pâté.

RULE 2
Any cat that hates beer but drinks it just to kill
the taste of the pretzels has a problem.

RULE 3
If you're letting the cat have a lick of beer so you can honestly
say you never drink alone, both of you have a problem.

RULE 4
When you notice your cat running in circles, chasing
two mice when there's actually only one, call the vet.

RULE 5
Cats are allowed to watch the dog
drink beer but not to mock him.

RULE 6
Just a guess, but Brut Champagne sounds
about right for a cat's choice of drink.

RULE 7
Although I like it, the New Zealand wine Cat's Pee on
a Gooseberry Bush would not be a good choice.

RULE 8
If your cat exhibits signs of being surly and standoffish,
he's probably not drinking. He's a cat.

RULE 9
If your cat has blurred eyes all the time, it probably
comes from staring at you all night long while you sleep.

RULE 10
Cats have a natural disdain for drink.
The same cannot be said, however, for marijuana.

14

The Cats of Key West

Cats are dangerous companions for writers, because cat watching
is a near-perfect method of writing avoidance.

DAN GREENBURG, AUTHOR

Cats—they sleep in the eavestroughs that run along the roof of his
second-storey writing studio; they sneak past the dozing custodian
and nap on his bed; they lounge by the pool and sun themselves on
the porches; they climb the palm trees in moments of rough play;
and they wander the overgrown tropical grounds with no hint of
weariness or worry, as if they own the place. And they do.

One impudent, overweight tabby even slips through the French
doors and jumps into the wood-and-leather Cuban cigar-maker's
chair that sits in front of the round gateleg table where he read and
corrected his copy or clacked away on his famous Royal typewriter
(although he preferred to write in longhand, standing at the
window). From the window, a calico glares out at camera-snapping

tourists with all the disdain she can muster and still stay awake.

They come here, these cats, to preen and sleep and play where humans are forbidden to tread, at the very altar of the Church of Ernest Hemingway, America's most deified writer ever.

Every day, hundreds of fans and curious travellers walk the grounds of the Hemingway Home and Museum at 907 Whitehead Street in Key West, Florida. None are allowed to actually enter such sacred areas as the writing room, the kitchen, and above all, the wine cellar in Key West's only basement. Except these cats, the residents. Sixty or maybe seventy-five cats—nobody's really sure. A roll call would be rude.

And nobody dares to show anything but affection and awe for the direct descendants of the world's most famous cat colony, the polydactyl felines of Papa Hemingway, who adored his domestic cats as much as he loved shooting wild ones in the green hills of Africa.

Although they all look like mutts, crossbreeds, and calicoes—and every combination in between—these are the legendary six-toed cats of the Pulitzer- and Nobel-winning author who lived in this large, forest green, two-storey Spanish-American house from 1931 to 1939. Here, he wrote 70 percent of his life's work, including the final version of *A Farewell to Arms,* the book that skyrocketed him to international fame, and to a level of idolatry never approached by any other writer … before or since.

I am told that a few of this coddled, carefree lot actually have seven toes, thereby upping the ante of their aristocratic, royal inbreeding. If the legend is to survive, some may have to develop eight.

These cats are special and spoiled, and they live their charmed lives in quiet, semi-private opulence during the day. At night, they can always vault the stone wall that secures the property and raise a little hell in the streets, exactly as Hemingway did.

One, a long-haired flaming red cat, has become a celebrity in his own right by regularly drinking from a urinal, the famous pisser from Sloppy Joe's Bar. The story goes that Hemingway was out on the prowl one night when he stumbled across a discarded urinal on Duval Street, in front of his favourite hangout, Sloppy Joe's. The washroom had been renovated, and the urinal sat at the curb waiting for the garbagemen.

Although he probably wondered the next morning why and how he did it, Hemingway wrestled this square porcelain pee tank onto his back and carried it through streets and alleys to his own backyard.

The urinal—embedded in a side garden between the main house and his guesthouse cum writing studio—became the watering trough for his cats. Aghast, his wife dressed it up with Spanish tiles and a huge Mexican earthenware urn, which today spills fresh water into the trough.

But it's still a urinal, and still the long-haired red comes at regular intervals to stand over the tiled, porcelain piece and sip cool water from the dripping, spring-like urn. Standing perfectly still and erect on two feet, engrossed in his task—just as his master wrote, standing at oversized windowsills in his study—he is a six-times-a-day photo op for tourists and the subject of the most popular postcard sold in the museum bookstore.

At the back of the grounds sits a clean, roughly constructed infirmary, with a set of cages to house sick cats away from the healthy ones while they receive veterinary care.

Yes, the six- and seven-toed cats that live in the house of Hemingway and help keep the legend of the master storyteller alive are special: the upper class of Key West Catdom. The grounds that once harboured the creator of *The Old Man and the Sea* are now the site of perhaps the most hallowed litter box on earth.

But on this island at the end of the continental American road, all things eccentric, especially cats, are looked upon as special.

It would be inaccurate to say that everybody down here owns a cat. Some residents on Key West have two, four, and six cats. The guidebook claims that Key West dogs are very well behaved. They have to be. They're outnumbered five to one by cats with retracting claws.

And the felines—asleep on the gingerbread porches and sprawled on car hoods everywhere—fit perfectly with the pace of the island's afternoons. As a blue leaps into a garden hammock, a motley Persian snuggles into the basket of a parked bicycle. The handlebars of this bike are festooned with a plastic pink flamingo, and the woman who rides it is a "white witch" with a long, flowing cape to match. It's Key West, man.

Across Old Town at Authors of Key West, a quaint compound of cottages and suites where published writers are given preferential treatment, I stay in the Hemingway Cottage, which comes with big-game antlers on the living-room wall, portraits of the writer in every room, early hardcover editions of all his books, and three cats that could but won't stay out of your lap.

I recall ordering only one on the phone—Leo, a small, black, six-toed scamp. But of all the cottages in this quiet and quaint bed-and-breakfast compound, which is much like the Hemingway house itself, the cats seem inextricably drawn to the one named for Papa. So Fat Billy, beige and really big, sleeps on the wicker sofa, while tiger-striped Alice, meek and polite, camps out on a deck chair on the porch. Erin, the compound's "fraidy cat," circles but never enters. Me? I have to sit on the couch inside and watch them through the screen door.

Billy sleeps and eats at Authors during the day, but at night, he dines at José's Cantina, a Cuban restaurant kitty-corner to the hotel. With annoying persistence, he has gone from sneaking in the back door to being welcomed at the front as the restaurant's official mascot.

Key West, the cat capital of America, where Hemingway lives on as king with his surviving entourage of multi-toed tomcats still very much in charge of the palace.

Odd that his cats have become the caretakers of this great American legend—the first writer ever to grace the cover of *Time* magazine—and not those who knew him best.

Martha Gellhorn, a great writer badly overshadowed by Hemingway's towering status—and, for a period of five years, one of his wives—called him "the greatest self-made myth in American literature."

Ouch! But you can't tell that to his cats.

CATTITUDE

*Kitty-corner: A popular intersection
for peeing and, therefore, sniffing.*

THE CAT RULES

As They Apply to Celebrities' Cats

RULE 1
"I'm a direct descendant of F. Scott Fitzgerald's cat.
My great-great-grandfather once tried to kill Hemingway's cat."

RULE 2
"Yeah, well, just because your old man makes a ton of money …
Wow! Are those real diamonds in your flea collar?"

RULE 3
"I was this far from shaking Socks's paw, but those
Secret Service cats are like the Gestapo, man."

RULE 4
"You were a Neverland cat? Please tell me
you bit Bubbles on the ass."

RULE 5
Sending care packages to Castro's cats only serves
to support his feline … sorry, fascist regime.

RULE 6
"Seriously, I'm God's own cat. We all are."

RULE 7
"I'd kill to be Oprah's cat.... That would be,
like, way cool. Ohmigod, hello!"

RULE 8
No cat, no matter the owner, is to be afforded special ...
"You're joking! First class with a window seat?"

RULE 9
"I have traced my family all the way back to 1620
in New Plymouth, Massachusetts. They were
the original Mayflower Mousers."

RULE 10
"You're Cat Stevens's cat? Yeah, right.
And I'm Federico Fellini's feline."

15

Weggie on My Left Wing

In the middle of a world that has always been
a bit mad, the cat walks with confidence.
ROSANNE AMBERSON, AUTHOR

It was a particularly bitter winter when the lake froze over with one loud crack. Ice particles floated for three freezing days on gentle waves, and then all at once, they became one clear surface from Morgan's Point to the Rathfon Inn. *Crack!* Suddenly, it was glass as far as you could see.

It snowed later that same night, and the deep freeze continued until five days later, when out came the neighbourhood kids with scrapers and sticks, one board, and two pucks.

The board straddled two large mounds of snow to become the bench where you sat to remove your boots and put on your skates. Two pairs of rubber boots became goalposts, and teams were chosen.

The absence of a fat kid made me both nervous and embarrassed. That's how we'd always started games on Mud Lake, in Dain City, where I grew up. The kid who weighed the most got selected first. "Go ahead, Lumpy. Show us your stuff."

And if Lumpy didn't crash through the new ice, the rest of us would quickly follow. Judging by this kind of leadership, I'm betting Lumpy is out there on the corporate conference circuit these days as a motivational speaker.

So I waited for the ice to be cleared and counted heads. Sure enough, they were one player short of two even teams. Out came the CCMs, the hockey gloves, and two sticks I'd had since my Juvenile days (no, not delinquent).

As I laced up my skates on the bench, a kind of bidding war for me began.

"We don't want him. You take him."

"You take him. He lives closer to you than us."

"Tell him we've got an age limit."

Ah, kids. You gotta love 'em. I made a mental note to trip the kid who made the old-age crack the first chance I got.

It wasn't long before the good ol' pond hockey game was in full swing. It was a puck-bouncing, skate-gnashing, stick-clashing, end-to-end chase scene, with four black rubber boots taking the brunt of the punishment.

Infractions were called out—"Hey, that was offside" and "Goal doesn't count"—and ultimately ignored. The score was routinely disputed until two different versions were being kept and loudly updated. Errant passes that went off the rink and down the lake were retrieved, after long shouts of "I'm not getting it. I got the last one. You shot it; you get it."

Appraisals were rendered and encouragement or discouragement offered: "You shoot like a girl. You're giving the puck away on pansy passes." And professional analyses of the game came quickly: "No wonder we're losing. No way you can score with your stick up your ..."

But I didn't let any of their remarks bother me.

That is, until I heard Derek say, "Uh-oh, here comes trouble."

Derek was the neighbour's kid, and he hadn't yet forgiven my cat for killing an oriole inside the family's bird feeder. He'd nicknamed Weggie "the Baltimore Strangler."

"Uh-oh," and suddenly, there he was, bounding through the snow like a miniature Lassie on his way to save the terminally moronic Timmy, who had climbed down an ice-fishing hole, believing it was a shortcut to Oz.

You don't often see a cat on a frozen lake, so play slowed and then stopped as all the kids watched Weggie slashing his way through the snowdrifts. Meanwhile, Derek delivered the highlights of my cat's rap sheet as if he were before a judge, arguing that the prisoner should not be released on bail. Except for the unfortunate Baltimore oriole incident, I felt kind of proud.

After the players were immobilized by curiosity, Weggie made his move. Over the mound of snow that served as the end boards he leapt, dashing past the rubber boots, cutting between six guys with stupefied looks on their faces. Then, rather savagely, he attacked the puck.

He pawed it, clawed at it, bit it, pushed it down the ice, and then repeated this gnashing assault on the black rubber disk until even Derek was laughing. As I watched him slip, slide, and lay a beating on the puck, all at the same time, I couldn't help wondering, Where did Tie Domi find the time to teach my cat how to play hockey?

But the amusement of watching a household pet play our national game gradually gave way to a lot of grumbling.

"This is stupid. Doesn't he have anything better to do? Like kill birds?" Derek was relentless.

I suggested we get rid of the hockey sticks and play the game Weggie-style.

"First team to push the puck with their foreheads through the opposing team's goalposts wins."

You'd have thought they heard a fish fart.

So I cleaned the snow off a square of ice next to the rink, picked up Weggie and his puck, and placed him in his own little arena. And he loved it. It gave him the traction he needed to launch an assault on the other puck, the one the kids were stick-handling down the ice.

So I placed him back on the small rink and then I placed him back on the small rink and then I … Man, this was getting old.

"That's it. Either the cat goes or I quit."

"There are no stupid cats in hockey." (Correct, which is why Weggie was a natural.)

Kids! So little appreciation of cat comedy.

"Why don't we use the cat for the puck?"

Okay, fun was over; time to go. So I hoisted Weggie over my shoulder and off we went, equipment and all, back to the house.

Longingly, he looked back at the boys, now a man short, going through the motions of a lacklustre pond hockey game.

A quick treat for the "Lake Erie Streak" and I was headed back to the rink when I noticed it had been abandoned. One kid ran back to fetch the second puck on the small square of ice as Weggie watched him from my bedroom window. He, too, was soon gone.

You won't see that on *Hockey: A People's History:* game called on account of a cat.

For one fleeting moment, I saw myself driving my little athlete to early morning practices and tournaments in other cities. But honestly, I don't think Weggie has a future in hockey. Although there's plenty of rock 'em, sock 'em violence in the game, there's just not enough killing to keep his interest.

CATTITUDE
Sitting in the catbird seat:
A winning position—unless you're the bird.

THE CAT RULES

As They Apply to Sports

RULE 1
To play an organized sport, a cat must develop a keen
attention span so as to … Hey! Yes, you! I'm talking to you!

RULE 2
So far, you've racked up 354 penalty minutes,
all for "delay of game."

RULE 3
No, they're not laughing at you.
It's the helmet that cracks them up.

RULE 4
It took almost a century for girls to earn the right to play
on boys' hockey teams. Don't get your hopes up.

RULE 5
Tree climbing against lumberjacks? Now *that* I can see working.

RULE 6
Don't get so excited. When the crowd chants
"Three Blind Mice," they're just making fun of the umpires.

RULE 7
What happened? The hotdog seller yelled
"Catsup" and you ran out to home plate.

RULE 8
Honestly, I'd get rid of the baseball bat
and think seriously about cat crokinole.

RULE 9
Yeah, the Minden Meno Paws would be
a great name for an all-cat hockey team.

RULE 10
No, sitting in the catbird seat is not the same
as sitting in the penalty box.

16

Tough as a Tuscan Cat

The clever cat eats cheese and breathes down rat holes with baited breath.

W. C. FIELDS

Five glorious and placid weeks in the rolling hills of Tuscany, northern Italy's lush corridor of thick forests and rich vineyards. The land of palms and scented pines, sun-dried tomatoes and hand-pressed olive oil—not to mention classic wines for under ten dollars a bottle. I should have been so happy.

And I was, except I was missing my pal Weggie, the arrogant little brat.

I know what you're thinking. Feeling guilty, eh, Bill, for leaving your buddy in a cage at the cat kennel for five weeks?

Hah! Weggie? In storage? That'll be the day. No, no, no. Weggie doesn't go to the vet's or the kitty care centre. No, Weggie is such an engaging little critter that he now has his own private house-sitters. Arlene and Brian adore this little bugger so much that if they don't get to house-sit him for a month or so, they send him gifts through the mail.

Believe me, folks, you don't need the Internet to find people as mentally soft as yourself.

So I was strolling around my rented villa near Castello di Modanella, thinking about how Weggie would punish me by pretending not to know me when I got back, and all of a sudden I heard him! "Meow!" It was his familiar sharp, demanding meow— the one that says, "Look at me. I'm bored, I'm hungry, I'm unappreciated, and what the hell have you done for me lately?"

"Meow!" It was his whiny, drawn-out meow. But it wasn't Weggie. It was an equally annoying and gorgeous little critter by the name of Do, pronounced *Doe*. Do, named after a popular musical note, was a white-faced, grey-patched male cat with the pinkest mouth and lips I'd ever seen. It was easy to see past his lips and into his mouth because Do never shut up. He was yapping even as he bumped across my shins to get my attention and rolled on his back in the grass to be petted. Do purred so loudly that he sort of choked when he stopped to inhale. Purr, choke, purr, choke—he sounded like my Miata idling on a bad batch of gas.

Do's whining was so incessant, so demanding, and so familiar that he instantly cured my homesickness. The only difference between Do and Weggie was that this needy little Italian con artist was screaming to get into my house instead of out of it!

Do saw me coming from a long way off, probably when I was clearing customs. Do was the villa cat, and with all the nearby properties filled on weekends with Romans escaping the city, there was never a problem for a professional mooch like him. But this was a weekday, and Do was between suckers … sorry, cat lovers, so to speak.

So I fed him and fussed with him and roughed him up and rolled him in the cool grass and made sure he had cold water. I quit giving him milk because he drank it so fast that I thought he might drown. For me, Do provided the one thing that was missing in my life at that moment—a daily dose of aggravation dressed in soft, warm fur.

Oh, there was one more difference between Do and Weggie: Do still had all his "wedding tackle," as my friend Dr. Dave likes to call it.

The story, as related to me by Cabriella, the villa manager, was that there were three cats at the castle—Do and two females, Re and Mi. I am not making this up.

During the day, Do left Re and Mi to live the pampered life up at the restored fourteenth-century castle of Modanella while he scrounged meals at two villas, two Tuscan hills apart. At night, Do would return to Re and Mi at the castle to make a little music, if you know what I mean.

Some nights, other male cats from nearby farms would wander their way to the castle to try out a couple of notes of their own, which was why Do's ears had more notches than Madonna's bedpost. Do was the resident orchestra leader. No guest maestro need apply.

It wasn't easy being a Tuscan cat—fleecing tourists and cadging meals by day, protecting and satisfying the musical harem at night. A half-hour sprawl in the warm afternoon sun, an hour's nap in the shade of a window well, and then it was back to pursuing a basic need or three.

At some point, Do abandoned me at the villa. I assumed it was just that time of the season—the spring music festival up at the castle, with Fa, So, La, and Ti in town.

I can't imagine Weggie surviving in the chaotic cat world of Tuscany. First of all, if his food isn't on time or just right, he goes off by himself and sulks. Also, begging is beneath him. Hell, asking politely is beneath him. Dinner is supposed to be there, and that's it.

And second, if Weggie wandered into the castle to find Re and Mi all alone, he'd probably ask them to sing something from the musical, like Macavity or Mr. Mistoffelees. Then he'd stretch back, close his eyes, and get the tar beaten out of him by Do, arriving home early from the villa across the valley.

You gotta be tough to be a Tuscan cat. It's not that Weggie doesn't have courage; he does. It's just that he's not ... well, equipped for that kind of macho muscle business.

In Weggie's Wainfleet Tuscan castle, he's not only the court jester and the resident eunuch, but also the king.

CATTITUDE

Fight like Kilkenny cats: Two cats in an
Irish pub talking about "the Troubles."

THE CAT RULES

As They Apply to Sex

RULE 1
Stop it. That's not even an attractive cushion.

RULE 2
I don't care who initiated it. He's a dog, stupid.

RULE 3
Yes, 'tis the season, but you're on the disabled list. Permanently.

RULE 4
Yes, she is beautiful, and no, the operation is not reversible.

RULE 5
All adult female cats are called queens. Don't even go there.

RULE 6
"Castration" is such an ugly word. I prefer to think
you were part of a Planned Parenthood project.

RULE 7
You can't even find Wind-Up Mickey. How are
you going to look after six active kittens?

RULE 8
Yes, it is true that a female's litter can have six
different fathers. You should be grateful you can
never be named in a paternity suit.

RULE 9
Okay, so his nickname is Thumper.
I wouldn't read too much into it.

RULE 10
I agree. The word "cathouse" is demeaning. How about:
"That guy couldn't organize sex in a feline bordello"?

17

My Cat Was Belled by a Bird

A dog is a dog, a bird is a bird, and a cat is a person.
MUGSY PEABODY, AUTHOR AND HUMORIST

Evil acts are committed in my neighbourhood. I know, because my patio serves as a makeshift morgue.

"Someone who murders repeatedly, often without motive, and usually follows a predictable pattern of behaviour." Yeah, that's him, all right. My cat is a serial killer.

Birds, bees, rodents, rabbits—anything that moves in a field, is smaller than a cow, and is not paying attention is fair game for Weggie.

He has cleverly organized his open-air dining menu according to the level of intelligence of the prey.

Stupid: Robins and starlings that fly into freshly cleaned windows and wake up to find themselves in a headlock. During spring's "silly season," when they're nesting and mating and jet-lagged from the long flight from the south, birds actually bump into each other in mid-air, causing cats to pause and roll their eyes before pouncing on the last one to get up.

Semi-stupid: Birds frolicking in my birdbath and having too much fun to notice a striped tabby approaching on his belly. I've seen neighbours running and screaming across my backyard, desperately trying to keep my birdbath from becoming a bloodbath.

Really stupid: Birds that fly into the neighbour's feeder, having not seen Weggie enter the aforementioned feeder earlier the same day. Imagine flying into a wooden feeding station for a little lunch and running smack dab into Weggie "Hannibal" Thomas, there for a little lunch of his own.

Smart and therefore rare: Hummingbirds, which dart away backwards at the last second, leaving Weggie swinging by his front paws on the hummingbird feeder with sweet, red water dripping down his face. He's no quitter, I'll say that for him.

Ever since Weggie arrived, birds around here have served as either nutritional supplements or home entertainment. Never have I considered using a bird as an automatic homing device to keep tabs on this murderous little tabby. Not until one sunny Saturday morning, anyway.

At eight o'clock that morning, Weggie bounded out the kitchen door, totally ignoring his breakfast bowl of dry pellets because he knew that within thirty minutes, over in the dense field down by the creek, he would have a little "frogs' legs and wings thing" happening.

But he no sooner hit the patio bricks than he was verbally assaulted by what I thought had to be a squirrel. It was a high-pitched, death-threat kind of nattering coming from a nearby maple tree. No matter which way Weggie turned, this excited jabber followed him, getting louder with each move. As I went around to the other side of the tree, I saw it. Shriller than an angry squirrel and bigger than a hummingbird—a tiny bird with a blue cap and the vocal cords of Sheila Copps.

What transpired next was something right out of the Keystone Kats. Weggie ran under the neighbour's pine tree, and the bird perched on its peak, nagging him all the way. Weggie ran under the neighbour's cottage, and the bird was waiting for him when he came out the other side. And he screamed blue bloody murder at him until he ducked back under to reconsider his position.

For a week, this natural alarm system hovered over Weggie's head like a police helicopter. Wherever Weggie went, the screamer was just an ear-splitting second away. It looked like a midget sparrow, or it could have been a small wren. It was probably a chickadee, but there was no doubt about its name: Beeper. That's right, I now had a Beeper for Weggie.

For several years, I'd been cowering behind trees and crouching in ditches, stalking and threatening Weggie to make sure he didn't go across the road. I'd pretty much undone the arthroscopic surgery I'd had on both knees by running full tilt to get between my cat and his would-be prey. Well, worry and wonder no more—finally I had a Beeper attached to the little bugger.

This was no nest-protection ritual, with the bird keeping the cat at bay. The chicks were long gone, and I had a sneaking suspicion that not all of them safely flew the coop. I believed at least one of them had met its demise at the claws of my cat, and this siren stalking was an ongoing act of revenge.

Beeper never really cared where Weggie went. His only job was to follow him and torment him every step of the way. Yes, this was a vengeance thing. Although I couldn't prove it, I believed the bird was a Sicilian species, and Weggie had eaten his eldest son. This was a family vendetta that was going to end only when someone's body was outlined in chalk on my patio.

Can you believe it? A bloody bird had belled my cat. It was Mother Nature's first venture into the electronic alarm business.

Beeper—I loved him—was like the bird world's equivalent of a parolee's ankle bracelet. Or, looked at another way, he was one more annoying new feature from Bell Telephone that I was somehow paying for but did not order. He was such a pest that he probably spent his winters causing false starts at the dog track in Hollywood, Florida.

My biggest fear was that Beeper would get just a little too close to his victim one day, and Weggie would have him for lunch with some f-f-f-fava beans and a nice Chianti. Then I'd have the whole damn family of Beepers descending on my house, seeking vigilante justice on me as well as my cat.

Anyway, for that moment, I was a happy man, and my new best feathered friend was my unlikely bird of paradise.

Meanwhile, Weggie was walking around as if the Mounties had his flea collar wiretapped and were sending me hourly updates. I knew where he was at all times—usually under the cottage next door with Beeper surveying both entrances.

Suddenly, when I wanted him home, there was no whistling or begging, no promising fresh liver or shaking the treat can. I just followed the sound of the embittered Beeper, and there was my guy, sitting on his haunches and glaring skyward.

Because I was able to locate him so easily, Weggie concluded that either I was psychic or he had badly underestimated my tracking abilities.

"Hi, Shortstop—beep! beep! beep!—ready to come home now?"

Like all good things, however, this too was to come to an end. Things took an ugly turn.

One day, I had to scrape a few drops of wet, white paste off the top of Weggie's head. I didn't have to take a sample down to the lab to find out what it was. But I knew Beeper had upped the ante of war.

As hard as I laughed, even I thought this was going too far. If he crapped on my cat one more time, I vowed, out comes the slingshot. And isn't that how all battles escalate into all-out warfare?

CATTITUDE

*Bell the cat: A new hi-tech program
created by Bell Telephone to bill pets.*

THE CAT RULES

As They Apply to Mother Nature

RULE 1
In the libertine land of nature, domesticated cats
have no right to kill anything. Period.

RULE 2
Okay, you can take a mouse if it's limping
or a bird with a broken wing. That's mercy killing.

RULE 3
Okay, and frogs that aren't leaping.

RULE 4
No, not a partridge preening.

RULE 5
Okay, your size or smaller, but no stockpiling.
You eat what you kill, and that's it.

RULE 6
Let's say that rabbit is below you on the food chain.
See that fox eyeing the rabbit? He's one step above you.

RULE 7
No, I will not help you drag it home.
If you can't lift it, you can't kill it.

RULE 8
If you think frogs' legs and pigeon sound disgusting,
never eat in a restaurant in Tangiers.

RULE 9
The crunching of bones is the worst sound you
will ever hear coming from under the porch.

RULE 10
For you, that is. For your cat, it's "rare mice pilaf."

18

The Cat, the Toad, the Call from Mom

Cat: a pygmy lion who loves mice, hates dogs, and patronizes human beings.
OLIVER HERFORD, POET AND HUMORIST

Question: Why did the cat cross the road?
Answer: Because I absolutely, categorically, and most emphatically forbid him to do so, that's why!

The battle over the dangerous demarcation line known as Lakeshore Road rages on between me and my cat.

At his disposal and with my blessing, Weggie has a half mile of beach on which to stroll, a creek with wild brush growing up both banks, and six summer cottages all conveniently raised on blocks for easy entry into and quick exit from the killing fields. The crawl-spaces of these cottages are rich with mice and moles. But not as rich as they were before the Caledonia Killer arrived. Yet Weggie insists on crossing Lakeshore Road into the woods because, in his words, "That's where the really big rodents roam, Bill."

In this war, I'm not even winning the odd battle. But I'm not quitting either, because I'm a guy, and guys, at least on paper, are supposed to be smarter than cats. (Most people would have quit when they saw what Weggie did on that paper. Not me.) And that is why our standoff on neutral ground was such a strategically important battle.

One day, I caught Weggie approaching but not crossing Lakeshore Road. By bolting behind four cottages and cutting up to the road behind a privacy fence, I was able to manoeuvre myself between him and the above-mentioned thoroughfare. Then I drove him back towards the house with two shots from my trusty Italian-made starter's pistol, like something out of *Rio Bravo*.

Showing exceptional speed for a slippered guy with two arthroscoped knees, I cornered Weggie under one of the cottages. Crawling on my belly to grab the little begger for the up-close-and-personal road lecture, I soon reached the point where I could go no farther. I was, so to speak, wedged in. But nor could Weggie get past me to escape.

We were getting ready for the long siege—which is usually called on account of darkness or supper—when out of the corner of my eye I noticed the toad, which I had also inadvertently cornered in my ambush.

This was a large toad, with warts the size of subway tokens and eyes that took up most of its head. When he blinked, it was like the hideaway headlights of a sports car popping up.

Weggie didn't see the toad until it took a quick, short hop. Instantly, the hunter instinct kicked in: he hunched down low as if it would make him invisible, thumped his tail, wiggled his bum, and … Just before he pounced, he remembered that little matter of the standoff with this really angry man with a gun. Me. The bum went still, and he sat up again, with a most unhappy frown on his face. Torn between his enemy and his prey, he looked as if he wanted some sort of ruling from a referee or a United Nations peacekeeper. This kill, he knew, would take some careful cat scanning. I could hear him whispering his own version of the "Beans, Beans, Beans" song: "Well, after you've been eating mice for a long time—toad, toad tastes fine." That's when all three of us heard the lady from Bell Telephone say, "Please hang up and try your call again. If you need assistance, dial your operator."

Weggie looked suddenly terrified, as if I'd abandoned the starter's pistol and called in an air strike.

I had pressed the portable telephone I carry in my shirt pocket into the ground and activated the On button. I have to carry the phone because even when I'm engaged in close hand-to-claw combat and trench warfare, it's in my best interests to maintain direct communications with my nearly ninety-year-old mother, who has recently taken to calling me Bobby.

Now all three of us—me, Weggie, and the toad—were staring at the telephone. There was no question that both of them needed assistance, but I was clearly in charge, now brandishing a gun *and* a talking phone.

And I think I could have settled things peacefully. I think I could have saved a toad and captured a cat. I think I could have walked out into the sea of television cameras and boom microphones and said, "Ah shucks, I'm no hero. I just done what any guy would have done."

If it hadn't been for that incoming phone call. *RINNNGGGGG*!

There followed a series of lightning-fast events that beg for slow motion, a pointer, and the narration of Don Cherry.

Spooked by the telephone, the toad made a series of quick, strong hops to get past me. Weggie, from a no-huddle offensive, sprang headlong at the toad. I snatched the toad out of harm's way. Clutching it with one hand, I grabbed Weggie by the scruff of his neck with the other. The toad peed all over my hand. Weggie screamed in terror and raked my wrist with his front claws. That's when I heaved backwards, bumping my head on a wooden beam just as my chest hit the ground and the On button activated.

"Bill? Is that you?"

It was my mother.

"Mom! Not now, please!"

"I was just wondering how you are, dear."

"I'm kind of busy at the moment, Mom, can I call you back?"

Weggie took a swing at the toad, which defended itself by emptying its bladder onto the cuff of my linen work shirt and all the way down my arm.

"Oh sure," she said. "I've got nothing better to do than sit here and wait for the phone to ring. You're the one with the life, dear."

"Mom, I'm in a bit of a jam here. Look, could you call John Grant, my neighbour, and ask him to come to Mary's cottage and pull me out from under it by the feet?"

"I suppose you think that's funny," she said before hanging up.

I lay there, wondering exactly how many notches I had just dragged men down on the animal intelligence scale. I was also wondering if you get warts from toad pee. Or does toad pee cure warts? I couldn't remember.

Then the Bell lady told me to please hang up and try my call again, so I let the toad go. He hopped past me with Weggie glaring at both of us. Then I kind of belly-flopped out from under the floorboards, banging my head on a couple of joists as I went. And like two wounded warriors—with pride taking precedence over the physical toll—Weggie and I went home. I think I learned a valuable lesson from it all—namely, that this crossing-the-road thing was making me crazy, and if Weggie kept it up, I was quite capable of seriously harming myself. Plus I realized I was not going to be nearly so handy with the starter's gun if my trigger finger broke out in warts.

CATTITUDE

Enough to make a cat laugh: Extremely funny,
like a one-eyed cat dressed as Lord Nelson.

THE CAT RULES

As They Apply to the Limitations of Embarrassing the Owner

RULE 1
A cat owner is required to dispose of dead mice. He is not obligated to pose with them for the cat's trophy photo.

RULE 2
A cat owner should get a ladder and retrieve the cat from the roof of the garage no more than four times in one day.

RULE 3
Okay, I'll pull you out from under the couch or the car, but I am not going under that cottage while those people are having dinner.

RULE 4
Why? Because I can't face him. You killed the cardinal that's been coming to his bird feeder for seven winters.

RULE 5
You still had red feathers sticking out of your mouth
when he came to the door. That's how he knows.

RULE 6
Snakes were never part of the deal. You scared
my mother right out of her rocking chair.

RULE 7
Don't you dare give me that look about my weight.
As far as you're concerned, it's just a bigger lap.

RULE 8
Do you somehow time your hairballs for the dinner hour?

RULE 9
Put that thing away. Didn't I have you neutered?

RULE 10
Oh, I know it's a goldfish. But whose?

19

Weggie—The Caledonia Carnivore

Night and day, in gentleness or cruelty, for better or for worse,
no other animal is as much of an extremist as the cat.

FERNAND MERY, AUTHOR

Spiders, toads, cats, mice, moles, birds, frogs, butterflies, rabbits, chipmunks, and a squirrel—my little Weggie might just be the cutest serial killer since Charles Manson.

I tell you, I did not know what a vole was until my cat dropped a dead one at the kitchen door. One day, he brought home something long and furry that nobody's ever seen before, and my fear is that it was the last reproductive member of its species.

A recent study revealed that more than five million birds a day are killed in North America by domestic cats. That statistic may be somewhat understated, though, because Weggie was in bed with a cold a couple of days last month. But still, it's a real problem.

I'm living with a dangerous psychotic. One moment he's breaking the neck of a wild rodent, and the next he's asleep in my lap, with his head in the middle of a book he cannot read.

When that batty Englishwoman pawned this little waif onto me, she described him in her letter as "handsome, intelligent, and very affectionate." And he is all of that. But if memory serves, those were also the words used by Ted Bundy's stepmother to characterize that serial killer the day before the state of Florida lit him up like a Christmas tree.

Mrs. Hallpike suspiciously omitted from Weggie's résumé the fact that he kills things at ten times the rate of your average carnivore, and five times faster than the lead character in any Freddy Krueger film.

And the really twisted part is that he eats two healthy meals a day at home. So he's not killing things for food; he's killing things for fun.

Don't get me wrong—I love him. But in the great outdoors, he's an evil little freak. He brings them all home, drops them in critical condition on the patio, screams to make sure I'm watching, then re-enacts Robert De Niro's torture scenes from *Cape Fear*.

Occasionally, I can throw a broom or a tea towel out the kitchen door and distract him just long enough to save a small life—or, more than likely, to grab the dying creature and mercifully dispose of it.

Once he knows he's got me cringing at the window, he scoops up the twitching quarry and runs like hell under the neighbour's cottage. It's the death dorm; only he comes out alive.

You've heard of England's House of Horrors? I live next door to the Cottage of Corpses. If the owner ever digs a foundation, he's going to think they built the place over a pygmy cemetery.

Weggie will most certainly be number one when they come out with the Cat Serial Killer Cards, unless they list the killers in alphabetical order. In Iraq, he'd be the ace of spades. He definitely fits the profile—cool, calculating, heartless. Remorse? After one good cat burp, he's asleep on my desk and snoring.

There's a saying that goes: "A cat wearing gloves catches no mice." Trust me, if it worked, both Weggie and I would be wearing idiot mittens every time he left the house.

And it seems he's moving up the ladder of predatory species. One day, the family four doors down woke up to find Weggie hiding in their bird feeder. The annoyed cottager called to remind me of his love of birds and also mentioned the fact that he doesn't let his kids watch that kind of violence on TV.

I went over to bring Weggie home, and there he was, up on the platform, hiding just behind the feeder with his paw to his mouth, signalling all of us to shut up. *You're scaring away the birds!*

I found the scene kind of amusing until a blue jay swooped down for a landing. Although he pulled off a collision-avoidance manoeuvre that earned applause from the small crowd gathered around the feeder, that bird will definitely be going back to nature as his primary food source.

As I pulled Weggie down and scolded him, he gave me his usual arrogant, condescending look—the same look the career crook Willie Sutton must have had on his face when he answered the question of why he robbed banks by saying, "'Cause that's where the money is."

This killing stuff is driving me crazy. Either I have to put a cowbell on the little fella, or I'll need to get my property rezoned as a lakefront game reserve.

I phoned Dr. David Thorne to see if there was a solution. "Would castration slow him down?" I asked. It seems I read about this somewhere.

"It would sure take the starch out of *your* shorts, wouldn't it?" he said.

He did have a point. Which is why men are so reluctant to have male pets neutered. It's the Bobbitt nightmare all over again.

Meanwhile, Weggie carried on killing everything that moved in the neighbourhood. And until he whacked the squirrel, his victims were—thank goodness—his size or smaller. But it occurred to me this morning that I haven't seen the lady who delivers my mail for about four days now.

I'm not accusing anybody of anything. It's just that she hasn't been seen in quite some time. Oh, I promise, I really do! Let the mail lady live, and I'll bell that cat as soon as the pet store opens in the morning.

I'm just hoping with all my heart that it's either a holiday weekend or a postal strike.

CATTITUDE

More than one way to skin a cat:
"Dithpicable," as Sylvester would say.

THE CAT RULES

As They Apply to Torture and Murder

RULE 1
I hope you *do* get warts; that toad wasn't bothering anybody.

RULE 2
Cats that kill for fun go to cat hell,
which is run by unleashed German shepherds.

RULE 3
No, the bell stays on the collar.
I'll tie another one to your tail if I have to.

RULE 4
If the bell doesn't work, you'll be wearing
a helmet with a motion-sensitive police siren.

RULE 5
One of these days, you'll pick on the wrong bird,
like a bald eagle. Skydivers call it free-falling.

RULE 6
You have to stop. I could be charged as an
accessory by the ones that are still alive.

RULE 7
The wildlife crime rate in Caledonia dropped
40 percent the day after you left.

RULE 8
Yes, two mice hanging from your mouth is a record.
It's also disgusting.

RULE 9
"It's the Little House of Horrors Museum on the phone.
They're looking for memorabilia."

RULE 10
No, there will be no Truth and Reconciliation Commission for cats.

20

Cats Are Quirky, with Near-Genius IQs

I love my cats because I love my home, and little by little, they become its visible soul.
JEAN COCTEAU, AUTHOR AND ARTIST

July is Adopt-a-Cat Month, and I would urge each and every one of you to do just that. You want to laugh, cry, bite your knuckles in frustration until they bleed? Get a cat. Better yet, get two.

They are, by far, the most fascinating domestic creatures on earth, and what's more, they're smarter than your brother-in-law. Sorry, *a lot* smarter than your brother-in-law.

Cats take part in an all-day, three-act play in the privacy of your own home. All you have to do is keep an eye on them. They're quirky and funky and surly, but to catch the really bizarre behaviour, you almost have to hide behind the drapes. If they know you're watching them, they won't perform—it's a union thing.

Strange as the expression "like fog on little cat feet" they are. And I have no idea what that means.

I have had cats most of my adult life, and I can assure you they are, at different times, more fun than TV and more soothing than a Cat Stevens ballad.

There was a time in my life when I lived with four cats. It was like Cirque Sans Soleil. They turned kitchen drawers into pullout couches, converted a one-bedroom apartment into four all-inclusive condo units, and took turns scaring the daylights out of one another. One would walk by a doorway and another would pounce just behind him, which would send the first one flying into the air like a spring toy, setting off the third one and then the fourth. I believe the Flying Wallendas developed their famous circus act by watching cats.

But that's not to say they're not helpful.

Weggie knows exactly what time I get up every morning, and he takes great pride in beating the alarm clock by fifteen minutes. A gentle tap to the nose with a soft paw beats a buzzer any day.

A couple days after I brought Weggie home, I caught him drinking out of the toilet. I asked my vet why would he do that when I always kept his water bowl filled. My vet told me that cats prefer the water in the toilet because it's colder in that particular bowl. From then on, I understood my cat a little better—it was the vet I really worried about. (How did he know the water was colder in the toilet?)

Cats are seeing more of the world these days.

Not long ago, a stray kitten stowed away in the air filter pocket of a Volkswagen Jetta for a harrowing three-hundred-mile trip to Chester Basin from Richibucto, in New Brunswick. Mac Walker found the kitten purring under the hood of his car at trip's end. The kitten was covered in grease and reeked of diesel fuel, but was otherwise in good shape. Walker kept the little urchin and, of course, named him Lucky.

Overland would've been my choice. One life down and eight to go. Lucky.

A two-year-old German cat by the name of Felix would consider Lucky's excursion a walk around the block. Felix escaped from her carrier in the cargo hold of a Boeing 747 flying from West Germany to Los Angeles. She hid aboard the jumbo jet, covering almost two hundred thousand miles and making sixty-four stops before she was discovered by airline workers.

Pampered by Pan Am on her return home, Felix enjoyed an in-flight meal of tuna and caviar while lolling on the lap of a flight attendant. It's called Pan Am's Executive Cat Class.

She even accumulated enough frequent flyer points for a free vacation in Hawaii.

People who believe cats cannot be trained have never seen the cat circus act on Key West's Mallory Pier at sunset. Walking on hind legs, performing back flips, jumping through hoops of fire—they're incredible to watch.

The truth is, you can get a cat to do almost anything as long as you're smart enough to preface your commands with the phrase "Don't you dare …" As in: "Don't you dare jump up on that couch!" "Don't you dare eat up all your dinner!" And, "Don't you dare walk away from me when I'm talking to you!" (This, I'm told, also works well when training new husbands.)

Dogs have a daily plan: the poop, the meal, the walk. Cats just make it all up as they go along. Dogs stick to the script; cats improvise.

And even after they pass away, a cat can create a real calamity.

A couple of years ago, a woman flew Qantas, Australia's national airline, from Melbourne to Sydney with her black cat stowed away in a carrying cage in cargo. When they unloaded the carrier from the plane, handlers discovered that the cat was dead.

Having been confronted by angry pet owners before, under similar circumstances, the freight manager at Qantas said, "No way. I am not going through this again."

So he advised the woman of a slight delay in delivery and sent an employee out to the local animal shelter to find a substitute. They quickly adopted a cat that looked exactly like the deceased—all black, no markings, a little on the chubby side.

The next day, the manager personally delivered the cat to the woman's home, bounding up the front steps, quite proud of his ingenuity.

"That's not my cat," said the woman immediately.

"Of course it's your cat," said the manager. "Yours was the only cat on the Melbourne flight; there couldn't possibly be a mixup."

"That's definitely not my cat," insisted the woman. "My cat was dead. I was just bringing him home for burial."

Even after they've passed on, cats are smarter than your average airport manager.

CATTITUDE

All cats are grey in the dark: Perhaps the stupidest of all cat sayings.

THE CAT RULES

As They Apply to Feline Intelligence

RULE 1
An adopted cat, in order to stay adopted, is not to
exhibit intelligence superior to that of his master.

RULE 2
Sorry. How about "owner"? No? "Handler"?
No, I will not refer to myself as your "human counterpart."

RULE 3
Get off the keyboard. Okay, so you
signed me in. That was just lucky.

RULE 4
Dumbed down? Nobody's asking you to act like a dog.

RULE 5
Okay, if the dog locks himself out and you flip
the latch to let him in, smirking is permissible.

RULE 6
Gloating is out of the question, even if you did
lock him out in the first place.

RULE 7
Do not give me that "Do the math" look.
I'll figure out the dosage myself.

RULE 8
Yes, we know you do nothing while everybody around you
busts their butts. You might want to keep it to yourself.

RULE 9
Dolphins are smarter than cats. Are too!
Are too! La-la-la-la-la … I'm not listening!

RULE 10
Don't even think about stowing away on a 747.
Have you not heard of *Snakes on a Plane*?

Weggie and the Invisible Fence

The obedient dog has to be taken for a walk. The headstrong cat walks alone.
DESMOND MORRIS, ANTHROPOLOGIST

In my ongoing quest to keep Weggie from being turned into a fur mat on the road in front of my house, I have enlisted the help of Dick and Tommy Smothers.

They are the spokes-brothers for the Invisible Pet Containment System, which is a terrific way of keeping your cat safe and secure within the confines of your property—provided your cat is a dog.

Their promotional material stresses the loving relationship between people and their pets with phrases like "man's best friend" and "member of the family." I kept searching for something that related to Weggie and me, like "the only crime is getting caught," or "innocent until captured on videotape," or "lower back pain from running through ditches chasing the wandering waif."

When I first received the brochure, I got quite excited about the concept of electronic pet containment. I imagined the equipment would include a steel chair with straps to hold the cat, a bright light to shine into his eyes, and a cattle prod for interrogation purposes:

Me: "So, Veggie, I understand you vent across zee road again today!"
No response.
Me: "LIAR!"
Zzzzzit!

I can just see the headline: Cat Kicks Cattle Prod, Owner Tasers Himself Unconscious.

But no, invisible fencing is a thin wire buried just beneath the surface of your property boundaries. According to the brochure, your pet wears a small receiver in his collar, and when he nears the buried wire, a small electric jolt stops him in his tracks. The more he challenges the end of your property, the more shocks he receives, and pretty soon, unlike a lot of husbands, he learns not to stray.

"Now, we've never actually tried it with cats yet," said the salesman who came out to the house. That cinched the deal right there. Weggie would be a pioneer, famous as the cat that did not go where others before him had gone—off property.

Weggie sat in the middle of the yard, watching the salesman and me pace off the property lines to get an idea of how much wire we'd need. He got excited. He thought it was a game. He started doing that weird sideways shuffle.

"I've never seen a cat walk like that," said the salesman.

Weggie followed us everywhere, never taking his eyes off us. Near the road, the salesman dug a hole to check the soil. Weggie stared at him with his head cocked, and you could tell he was thinking to himself, This must be some kind of a trap.… Probably a chain-link fence, or maybe even an invisible live wire buried just below the surface of the soil, so when I come charging across, wearing a small receiver collar …

Okay, he may not have figured everything out, but he is a damn smart cat.

He followed us the length and breadth of my lot with the suspicious, conniving eyes of … well, a cat.

"There could be a couple of problems with a cat," said the salesman as we stood on the kitchen patio.

A couple of problems with this cat!

Trust me, with Weggie, I have problems indexed by subject matter and cross-referenced by the severity of the consequences. Example: *Hydro pole climbing—zero chance of survival if he does his tightrope walk on the live wire.*

With Weggie, the words "a couple of problems" are music to my ears.

"He could go over the fence," said the salesman.

"How does he know where to jump if the fence is invisible?" I asked. (Hey, I didn't fall off the back of the turnip truck that brought me here. I rode shotgun.)

"Cats can climb trees, ya know," he said.

No kidding, Sherlock. I spent one Sunday morning on a wobbly extension ladder after Nukey, the neighbourhood Husky, broke his rope and decided to send Weggie to a place where only skydivers have gone before.

"Or he could run across the electronic line, and then he'd get a jolt when he tried to get back onto the property," said the salesman.

I was beginning to think the Smothers Brothers really did invent this thing.

"You mean"—I really was trying to grasp the concept—"like an escaped convict from Millhaven electrocuting himself on a high-voltage fence while trying to break back *into* prison?"

"I don't know about a convict," he said. "I deal with dogs."

"I do deal with a convict," I said. "That's why you're here."

"Tell me," I said, "will this hidden wire give a shock to people walking across my property, like the guy who reads my meter or the Bell repairman or neighbourhood kids?"

"No, they'll be immune to the signal," he said.

"What if I pay extra for that feature?" I asked.

The salesman was starting to get annoyed.

I was pretty much sold on the system when we sat down at the picnic table in the backyard to finalize the details. Pretty simple—an underground wire and a power pack that delivers the electric stimulus that would discourage my cat from crossing the property lines.

Just then, Weggie came bounding up onto the picnic table to make sure the record would show that he was present at the meeting but did not sign anything.

As far as I was concerned, it was a done deal. A day to dig was set and two dates for payments arranged. On that pleasant day by the lake, the three of us sat enjoying one another's company in a triangle of deceit.

I was about to agree to have my cat mildly tortured; the salesman was about to cinch a sweetheart deal on a piece of property that is 150 feet long; and Weggie, the innocent patsy in this plot, would, I knew, win out in the end. Cats are far more intelligent than men, especially when one of them is Tommy Smothers.

As an afterthought, I asked to see the collar, a royal blue nylon strap with a matching plastic power pack.

I liked it. Nice, neat, and bright enough to be spotted easily in the grass. It had heft to it that spelled expensive.

I scooped Weggie off the picnic table, dropping him gently to the grass.

"Let's see what it looks like on him," I said.

"You know, it's not connected or anything," said the salesman as he put the electronic collar on the cat and tightened the strap around his neck.

Weggie began walking in circles, with his neck tilted to one side.

After a couple of turns, the power pack was dragging on the ground, along with Weggie's left ear.

In ever-smaller circles he went, the power pack now bouncing over the lawn. He tried to paw it off but couldn't, because although his body was upright, his head was weighted down to the ground. He looked like a mechanical cat whose battery was running low.

I was laughing so hard that I started to tear up, and despite seeing his sale go down the proverbial drain, the salesman was absolutely hysterical as well.

Every time he tried to knock the power pack off with his paw, Weggie tipped over. It was the funniest damn thing.

Who knew technology could produce such great situation comedy?

I mean for a large dog—say, from Newfoundland—this electronic unit could be considered a "small" collar. For Weggie, a cat who weighs ten pounds when he's soaking wet from being chased through the ditch by a guy yelling, "Get back up to the house, you little &%$#*!"—well, it felt more like the spare tire off a pickup truck.

The collar weighed three pounds.

As he circled in front of us twice more, I thought I heard a muffled "Take it off, Bill. Take it off now! I mean it!"

The salesman was stunned. So I mumbled something about being a bit of a ventriloquist. The salesman hadn't laughed so hard since Tommy Smothers told him that even *his* mother loved him best.

Finally, in the middle of all this lakeside mayhem, it dawned on me.

"It works," I yelled. "It really works!"

I think the real source of my excitement was the hundreds of dollars I'd just saved. I realized that I didn't need an invisible fence. I just needed a three-pound anchor strapped to my cat's neck. Weggie wasn't going anywhere with that bright blue albatross around his throat. If he ever crossed the road again, it would have to be in small, slow circles.

"How much for just the collar?" I asked.

By this time, the salesman was packing everything into his briefcase, having come to the conclusion that cats cannot be fenced in, invisibly or otherwise. I wasn't so sure.

"Send me the seven-pound collar!" I yelled as he was getting into his car. "With that one, he won't even be able to leave the house!"

Weggie, as I knew he would, prevailed in the end. Felines defy the electronic fence, and except for those brief periods of pure pet slapstick, you can't keep a good cat down.

CATTITUDE

Like herding cats: Or trying to get parrots to fly in formation.

THE CAT RULES

As They Apply to Neighbourhood Roaming

RULE 1
Cats are not to leave the property, under any circumstances.

RULE 2
Okay, the cat can venture just across the property line to pee
in the miserable guy's flowerbed and return immediately.

RULE 3
Okay, the cat can go under the other neighbour's cottage
to kill mice, which would be doing her a favour.

RULE 4
No, the creek is farther than five cottages down. That's too far.

RULE 5
Okay, okay. If you promise not to go to the barn
to hunt rats, you can go to the creek to kill frogs.

RULE 6
Yeah, I heard about the mole problem in Dunnville.
No, cats do not hitchhike.

RULE 7
No, make do with the dead fish. You're not getting a boat.

RULE 8
You keep humming "Home on the Range"
and you'll go without supper.

RULE 9
I found a road map in your toy box. Don't make me use leg irons.

RULE 10
Yes, I did hear about the cat that walked five hundred miles to his
owner's new house. He also missed 136 regular meals, stupid.

22

Cat People versus Dog People

Cats are the ultimate narcissists. You can tell this because of all the time they spend on personal grooming. A dog's idea of personal grooming is to roll around on a dead fish.

JAMES GORMAN, AUTHOR AND SCIENTIST

Recently, after reading a story I wrote about Weggie, a subscriber to *PETS Magazine* sent me a letter that began: "Dear Foolish Feline Freak …"

True or not—as I tell the students in my writing seminars—we should always attempt to avoid annoying alliteration.

This is not the only time I've been accused of crossing that line in the sandbox from dogs to cats and back again. To this point in my life, I have lived with both cats and dogs—six felines and three dogs, to be exact—and I've noticed that they are exceedingly different.

It goes without saying that cats and dogs are as different as night and day, which would make excellent names if you had one of each (the dog, of course, being Day).

Having cohabited with both, I couldn't help noticing that dogs are … okay, dumber. And as a typical guy, I'm just naturally more comfortable in that environment. I love the drooling flattery of a dog as much as I do the measured standoffishness of a cat.

It's odd that animal behaviouralists believe dogs can understand several hundred words, while a cat is limited to fifty (and usually appears to understand a lot fewer than that). Apparently, cats don't need to be verbose to control your house and their world the way a dog never could.

Generally speaking, cats are smaller and more cynical; dogs are bigger and more naïve. A cat is a clever little creature that can often make a guy look stupid. A dog, however, can flatter a man by embracing and rejoicing in his stupidity.

Like at midnight, if the fridge door hits you in the arm, knocking the plate of leftovers and sending the quart of milk crashing to the floor, the dog doesn't ask what or why. He's immediately and enthusiastically involved in the cleanup. A cat, on the other hand, will sit and analyze the situation: looking at you, looking at the mess, looking eminently superior. Yes, despite what you may have heard, a cat will, in fact, worry over spilled milk.

Resourceful? Try leaving your dog home alone overnight with a bowl of food, a dish of water, and a nice, clean litter box.

If you ask a cat, "Jawannagoferawalk?" you get nothing in return. The cat will just burrow even deeper into the pillow of the couch.

But before he nods off, he'll give you one weird, last look, as if you need a thorough psychological assessment, the kind that involves a whole team of doctors with thick, round glasses.

But if you ask a dog, "Jawannagoferawalk?" he exhibits behaviour similar to that of Richard Simmons with a colony of piss ants in his pants. He's wild with exuberance. He's animated. He's outta here!

Dogs will follow you into a ground war in a Pacific jungle if your request begins with "Jawanna." On the other hand, it takes a week for the scratches on your arms to heal after you get your cat to the vet's.

Dogs are like drunken frat brothers—followers, joiners, good-time Charlies. Cats are like Howard Hughes—weird and eccentric, with very long fingernails.

Dogs attack mailmen; cats attack mice. I have no idea what that means.

Dogs are like Shriners in a parade—fun-loving, go-cart-driving, impossible to embarrass. Cats are like paramedics at rock concerts. It's prudent to have them nearby; they're just not part of the party.

If you watch television with a dog and turn it up loud when Eddie on *Frasier* starts barking, the dog will get excited and bark back. If you watch television with a cat and turn it up loud when Garfield is on the screen, the cat will turn down the volume and then switch the channel to PBS's *Masterpiece Theatre*. A dog is a lump on the couch in the den. A cat is a critic of both lumps on the couch in the den.

If you're reading or writing, a dog will take that opportunity to sleep at your feet. If you're reading or writing, a cat will take that opportunity to get between you and the page.

A dog is like your silent but disinterested partner in crime. He doesn't care what the caper is, as long as things are happening and he's involved. A cat is like a union steward. He also doesn't care what you do, as long as you do it his way. Otherwise, don't involve him.

Dogs smell each other's butt as a form of identification. A cat will make note of the name on the other cat's collar and have the lineage traced later.

Cats are fastidious, wary, worrisome, and usually skinny. Cats are like Calista Flockhart. Just try giving a cat a pill. It's "Why should I take the pill? What's in the pill? Will the pill cause such sudden weight gain that when I stand sideways, I'll actually be visible?" Giving a cat a pill is like a day-long horking marathon, with the whole bottle eventually dissolving into a big ball of spit in your hands. You could molecularly bind that pill with Beluga caviar and it would still come out of that cat's mouth like candy from a Pez dispenser. Trust me, anybody who has ever tried to get a cat to swallow a pill winds up wondering if it would work at the other end.

Dogs, on the other hand, are a lot like Jack Klugman. Give him a pill that's been rubbed in anything resembling food, and a dog will have just one comment on the whole procedure: "Gulp!" And then he'll sit and wiggle his bum, which says, "Gimme another one, Bill. I've been a good boy today."

Dogs make great companions. Cats make very good company managers.

And there it is, right there: With a dog, you're family; with a cat, you're staff and on contract.

Dog people are social animals who love to meet others on their daily walks. Cat people choose instead to read by the window with the cat napping on the sill, both shaking their heads as the canine parade passes by.

Dog people are needy. They fumble with the key in the lock because they're so excited by the grand wagging welcome that's happening on the other side of the door. Cat people go easy with the key because they don't want to wake anybody up and find themselves in sulk city.

Dog people are careless and often display mustard stains on their shirts. Cat people are fastidious and often notice that the fabric with the mustard stains is less than 40 percent cotton.

Dog people believe in the master/pet relationship. Cat people do too, but it's reversed, eh?

Dog people are pack animals who enjoy and need the company of others. Cat people enjoy nothing more than a nap and a cuddle with a cat.

People who want love are dog people; people who want to give love are cat people.

CATTITUDE

Look what the cat dragged in: A dishevelled, somewhat unstable being; usually a puppy or your brother-in-law.

THE CAT RULES

As They Apply to Dogs

RULE 1
Big is dumb. Small is smart. Get that straight,
Sparky, and you get to keep your nose.

RULE 2
Everything—drawers, closets, chairs, couches, windowsills—
is the cat's. See all that space beyond the window?
That's yours, big guy.

RULE 3
It's called "self-cleaning." It keeps me out of hot water.

RULE 4
Cat can. Dog can't. Ah, that's why they call it *fur*-niture.

RULE 5
I don't care if they love you more than they love me.
I'm all about respect.

RULE 6
She did not attack you. Maybe she just
felt like going for a doggie ride.

RULE 7
She did not tinkle in your water bowl. You're just paranoid.

RULE 8
She beat you down the stairs 4,858 times in a row.
Why do you keep trying?

RULE 9
Look, they neutered us both. You can forgive; I never forget.

RULE 10
Notice that they haven't had many visitors
since you and I arrived. Stick to the plan.

23

Weggie Did the Crime and Got Off Scot-Free (This Time)

A cat is more intelligent than people believe, and can be taught any crime.
MARK TWAIN

I am not a paranoid person, although there are days when I believe Weggie is a space alien on a mission to test the limits of human patience on earth.

One morning, I was on my usual Weggie patrol—pacing up and down that section of Lakeshore Road between my property and the field across the street. It's busy on summer weekends, and I was training him not to go near it.

Much like a stupid bank robber, I was wearing bright clothes and no mask; I had a gun and a pocket full of rocks.

The plan was to spot him before he got over the road. As he wearily approached the road he knew he wasn't supposed to cross,

I would fire the starter's pistol twice to scare him, then hurl two rocks behind his frantically fleeing bum to let him know I meant business. Although this scheme never actually worked that way, that's never stopped me from trying.

The fear that I would one day be scooping his tire-treaded body off the road kept this plan viable, not to mention dangerous. For me, not him. A few days earlier, a policeman had driven by very slowly. Had he noticed my gun, and jumped out and drawn his own, you'd now be reading about the most one-sided duel in recent history.

After twenty minutes of pacing, I assumed a menacing position, gun at the ready, right beside the north end of the creek that runs from the field under the road and into the lake.

By this time, I figured Weggie had probably spotted me and decided not to try to run the border. Instead, he'd likely gone to the south end of the creek along the beach side, which is fine.

But Weggie's favourite hunting ground is a spot where the field banks down the creek. That's where the mice, birds, bugs, frogs, and guppies come together. For Weggie, it's like the all-you-can-eat chicken-and-seafood special at Red Lobster.

So I was still guarding against his making a run for the field when I heard some rustling behind me and turned around to see him on the bottom of the dried-up creek bed, across the road. Across the road he was forbidden to cross.

"How can this be?" I asked myself, out loud, as would any guy armed with a gun and trying to wrangle a cat. "I was standing at the side of the road all this time! He could not possibly have got past me. Not without the help of David Copperfield and a cat box with a secret trap door."

After analyzing the situation carefully and considering his arrogant stare, I realized that he did not go over the road. He went *under* the road. The exceptionally hot summer had dried up the end of the creek. Unbeknownst to me, Weggie, little deviate that he is, had once again beaten the system.

Our deal was that he was never, under any circumstances, to go over this thoroughfare. So by simply walking up the creek and at the last second ducking through the culvert—in effect, going under the aforementioned venue to the party of the second part, subsequent to an appeal by a court-appointed arbitrator to determine wrongful house arrest by the plaintiff in this case—the little bugger had found a loophole in the law.

Apparently, for most of the summer and all of the fall, Weggie had been crossing the road in a technically legal manner.

I was looking straight at him when he put a paw up in the air. "Oh sure," you say. "He was simply jabbing at a spider in a web." But I could swear I heard him say, paw raised, "Not guilty, Your Honour."

All sorts of things started racing through my mind.

Is there such a thing as a cat lawyer, for instance? And even though Weggie was guilty as sin, would I have to sit through some sort of kangaroo court, listening to a sleek feline attorney throw catching little rap lines at me: "If he went under, then it's your blunder," or, "If there's justice for the meek, then you're up the creek."

Exactly how smart is this cat? I wondered. As he sat there practically waving at me, I began to imagine that he was the only cat alive that would someday be charged with flea-collar crime—and get off.

I started thinking back to other suspicious circumstances, like the day he came home with two mice dangling from his mouth. (Honest, I have a witness.) Now I was wondering, Was he in the middle of killing the first one when the second one surprised him? Blood on the patio, cat hair on the mice—if Weggie wore socks, I'd probably find them on the bedroom floor.

Anyway, I started down the bank to grab him, and he bolted straight through the culvert, back to the legal side, our side of Lakeshore Road.

I cocked my arm to give him a couple of noisy incentives, but I stopped when I heard a squeaky little voice say, "I would not, could not, and did not do this crime!"

Oh, he did it, all right. He crossed the line.

But as any good pet psychologist will tell you, punishment is effective only if you see him do it and punish him right on the spot.

Or as the foreman of the jury would say, "Oh, he probably went under, but the whole thing makes you wonder."

Ten minutes later, he was sitting at the window of opportunity … sorry, the door, acting as if nothing had happened.

Oh yeah, he did it, all right. He knows he did it. I know he did it. We *all* know he did it. And there's not a damn thing that can be done.

Crime and punishment—sometimes they just miss each other, for no good reason at all.

CATTITUDE

A cat has nine lives: A cat has but one life;
Shirley MacLaine has nine.

THE CAT RULES

As They Apply to Legal Issues

RULE 1
Cats are not allowed in courts of law.
They make lawyers feel less devious.

RULE 2
Judge: "Bailiff, please have the witness
removed from under my robe!"

RULE 3
"Your Honour, my client sprayed his own
character witness. That can hardly be intimidation."

RULE 4
When the bailiff says, "Put your paw on the
Bible and swear," don't say the S word.

RULE 5
"Whatever" is not a reasonable response
to all the questions they asked you.

RULE 6
Judge: "No, keep the bell on him.
The owner must know something we don't."

RULE 7
Judge: "Would legal counsel please remind his client, the cat, that
he can plead guilty or not guilty. He cannot plead for a treat."

RULE 8
"No reflection on the court, Your Honour.
My client just sleeps a lot."

RULE 9
Judge: "So your defence is that this crime—like every
crime ever committed—was carried out by a dog?"

RULE 10
"The cat's got my tongue." Now that one I like.
If the judge has a sense of humour, you're home free.

24

Weggie's O. J. Moment

A cat has absolute emotional honesty: human beings,
for one reason or another, may hide their feelings, but a cat does not.

ERNEST HEMINGWAY

There are days when I believe the word "catastrophe" comes from the word "cat," the cause of the event, and the word "trophy," the fact he's proud of it.

After two weeks touring Portugal with my brother-in-law, Danny, I tried to take my own life.… No, I tried to call home to check on Weggie.

The day before our flight home, I found myself sitting on the proverbial sun-drenched patio in Portugal (to be honest, though, there were some axiomatic clouds closing in from the west), and the waiter approached the table with a phone. My call home to check on Weggie had finally been put through.

From the moment my house-sitter said hello, I knew something was wrong.

"Is Weggie okay?" I asked.

"Yeah, Weggie's fine," she said breathlessly. "But it looks like O. J. Simpson may have murdered his wife."

O. J. Simpson? Murder? His wife?

"Carolyn, I thought I told you: NO WILD PARTIES!"

"No, it's in L.A. Some kind of car chase."

Suddenly, I too was talking in panicked, hushed tones.

"Well, is O. J. headed north to Wainfleet, for God's sake? Did he leave some kind of note? Did he mention Weggie by name?" I asked. I know this cat can irritate just about anyone, but O. J. Simpson? "Is this guy totally out of control, or what?" I asked.

"Actually, he's in a white Bronco on the San Diego Freeway," she said. "I'm watching the chase on TV."

"You're watching the chase on TV?" I repeated.

"Yeah," she said. "They're televising the chase live on all the major networks."

I thought for a moment. "You know that one key I left you? The one I said you should never use? The one that opens the liquor cabinet?" I asked. "Carolyn, you didn't use that key, did you?"

"No, no. They're chasing O. J. all over the L.A. freeways. It's been on for about half an hour."

"The chase has lasted half an hour?" I asked.

"Yeah," she said. "But they're only going, like, forty miles an hour."

I thought to myself, Of course the chase could go at only forty miles an hour. How else could the colour commentators have time to do their voiceover?

I was still confused, but I decided to take a shot. "Do you think O. J. knows that if he went faster, it would be a better chase and he'd actually have a greater chance of escaping?"

"Actually," she said, "O. J.'s in the back seat with a gun."

That's not so unusual. I've driven on the freeways in L.A. But the fact that he was steering and working the pedals from the back seat—well, that explained why the best he could do was forty miles an hour. Now it was starting to make sense.

"There must be twenty cops chasing him," she said.

I was paying for this call, so I took another shot. "From what you know so far, do you think the cops realize that if they went faster, it would be a better chase and they'd have a greater chance of catching him?"

"There must be twenty helicopters chasing him, too," she said.

"The cops are chasing him with helicopters?" I asked.

"No, no, no. The cops are chasing him in cars. The reporters are chasing him in helicopters," she said.

"At any time, have they cut away to Steven Spielberg sitting in a director's chair with a megaphone?" I asked.

"No, but there are people on the overpasses, and they're waving and cheering," she said.

"Are you sure it's not just an ad for Hertz?" I asked. "Like a new preferred customer protection plan or something?"

"I don't think so," she said. "One commentator said that O. J. might shoot himself right there in the back seat."

Hey, I write for television. That can't happen. If he kills himself, that's the end of the chase scene right there.

Then, Carolyn mentioned something about a witness, a free-loader sleeping on the couch.

To which I replied, "Hey, c'mon. Don't be so hard on yourself."

That's when the phone got cold and clammy in my hand.

"Listen, how's Weggie?" I asked. And that's when the line went dead.

Great. It cost me fifty bucks to phone home to listen to a house-sitter, who obviously had been into my single-malt collection, describe to me a celebrity episode of *TV's Bloopers and Practical Jokes*.

I went back to the room and told Danny, and he looked at me as if the green wines of Portugal had finally taken their poisonous toll.

When I woke up the next morning, I thought maybe I'd dreamed the whole thing. Two days later, at the airport in Lisbon, I spotted a group of Canadians coming off the Canada 3000 plane that we were taking back. I approached a guy wearing a Blue Jays cap.

"How're the Jays doing?" I asked.

"Awful," he said. "Hey! Did you hear about O. J. Simpson?"

Lord, it was true—the chase, the cops, the live coverage, the …

"Uh, look," I said in a very low voice, "this may sound kind of silly, but there wasn't a cat involved in that thing, was there?"

"Nah, I don't think so," he replied. "But there was something about a dog with blood on his paws."

CATTITUDE

Queer as a cat fart: Incredibly strange,
like the plots of all John Irving's novels.

THE CAT RULES

As They Apply to Trials of the Century

RULE 1
Cats may be called to testify in certain high-profile cases,
provided they can play teeter-totter on the scales of justice.

RULE 2
During cross-examination, a cat can lie
under his breath, but not under oath.

RULE 3
Cats make great jurors for the guilty because
they can relate to random killing.

RULE 4
Having said that, even twelve cats would have found O. J. guilty.

RULE 5
Kato is a fine name for a cat; it's just not a great name
for that professional mooch sleeping on your couch.

RULE 6
When cats become lawyers, dogs will join
the long list of the wrongly accused.

RULE 7
It's hard to say if Jean Harris was fond of cats.
She sure didn't like diet doctors!

RULE 8
Oh sure, Saddam abused cats too,
but that still didn't justify the invasion.

RULE 9
News report: "On the stand today, two Neverland cats
testified that Michael Jackson was one weird dude,
but he never mistreated the animals."

RULE 10
No, I'm pretty sure that Robert Blake had a pet parrot, not a cat.

25

When the Vet Hangs Up the Rubber Gloves

Everything I know, I learned from my cat. When you're hungry, eat. When you're tired, nap in a sunbeam. When you go to the vet's, pee on your owner.
—GARY SMITH, AUTHOR AND HUMORIST

Normally, it's a sad day when your vet hangs up the rubber gloves and hands his stethoscope over to a younger man in white. However, when my vet, David Thorne, decided to call it quits after thirty-one years of poking and groping cranky pets, many people were still slapping their knees in laughter.

A gentle and caring man of medicine, the Marcus Welby of the pet world, David graduated from the Ontario Veterinary College in Guelph and took a job in Wingham, Ontario, to administer to large farm animals. He promptly bought himself a brand-new, two-door, hard-top Dodge Coronet. Something in the air—probably the smell of two bloated and rotting two-hundred-pound pigs in the trunk—must have told him it was going to be a rather curious career.

Eager to make a good impression, David decided not to wait for the truck from the dead stock company and instead drove the animals—which had succumbed to dysentery—to the lab in Guelph for post-mortems. Not exactly that new car smell most of us proudly inhale. The car was never quite the same.

After four years of working at both ends of large animals, David moved to Port Colborne, Ontario, where he hung out his shingle at the Clarence Street Veterinary Clinic. There followed a series of incidents so strange that it almost made him long for his days with those two past-due pork chops in the back of his car.

Like all vets, David has been amazed to see what comes out of our pets—golf balls, fish hooks, washcloths, open safety pins, and 434 one-inch stones from a boxer that tried to eat his own enclosed run. David has removed two pieces of flip-flops from the same cat—twice—and a ten-inch rubber bat from a black lab.

The motor mount that came out of the Rottweiler was highly unusual, but the eighteen occasions he had to remove porcupine quills from a male German shepherd in Wingham and the fourteen times he repeated the procedure on the female partner … well, that was downright discouraging. (The numbers would indicate that the female was beginning to smarten up.)

Surprised were the owners who brought in their cats, yowling in pain, only to be told they were actually advertising the fact that they were in heat.

Very surprised was the overworked dogcatcher who nabbed a stray dog and immediately brought him to David's clinic because the animal was limping.

"But he's only got three legs!" exclaimed Sherry, David's assistant, in the waiting room.

"Oh, so he has," replied the city worker as he and Tripod made a quick exit.

To this day, David still marvels at the man who brought his dog to the clinic on four different days, each time using a rather unusual leash. The first time, he showed up with an extension cord around the dog's neck. The next time, it was a microphone cord with the microphone still attached. Then a plumb line—the kind builders use to line up boards—and finally, an adapter cord for a cigarette lighter. Only the dog appeared to be embarrassed.

And then came a woman with a dog that her son claimed had given him a bad dose of crabs. When David explained that this was not possible, it was difficult to tell whether the mother or the dog was more relieved. (A great way to escape such an embarrassing situation would have been for the mother to say, in her best Inspector Clouseau accent, "But of course, that's not my son!")

We all hope for comfort and consolation at the vet clinic, but nobody was more relieved than the man who brought his dog to David and was told it suffered from a urinary tract infection. The dog slept in the couple's bed, between them, and every morning there was a yellow stain on the sheets.

"Thank God," the man announced to a crowded waiting room. "I thought it was the wife."

When the staff of vet clinics suddenly rush to the back of the building, it's not always a real emergency. Sometimes those rooms behind closed doors serve as a place to politely laugh your head off.

Particularly peculiar was the case of the budgie that insisted on humping a little ball in his cage. The bird was obsessed with the little red ball, and the pseudo-sexual activity was constant. The vet and the seventy-year-old man who owned the bird concurred. Their diagnosis? That was one horny budgie humping away in that cage.

However, they completely disagreed on the solution. David suggested they simply remove the ball from the cage, while the old man, not wanting to ruin all his pet bird's fun, suggested they drill a tiny hole in the little red ball and … Well, you get the picture.

Yes, David has seen it all. During three decades of veterinary medicine, he has been bitten by dogs, peed on by cats, and kicked by cows. Once, he even slit his wrist while castrating an uncooperative steer.

But no vet in his entire career has had a moment more harrowing or hilarious than the one David faced while performing surgery on the anal area of a German shepherd one day. David dropped the scalpel, the scourge of all surgeons. Laden with bacteria, it stuck straight into his thigh, and a stream of blood shot up through his pants.

"It was bleeding pretty bad," he recalls. "I thought it must have cut my femoral artery."

The operating room staff was in panic mode, and David's two female assistants looked on helplessly. The scalpel did not sever the artery, the bacteria did not cause infection, and once David drove himself to emergency, everything turned out fine.

However, he'll never forget the sight of his two assistants standing there in the operating room, alternating between horror, shock, and nervous giggling. Through all the pain and panic, they couldn't help thinking that in order to save their boss's life, they just might have to pull down his pants.

It may not seem like a great tribute to a long and wonderful career, but let it be said that in thirty-one years of saving lives, David Thorne never once dropped his pants.

Congratulations, David. And for your kind manner and brilliant way with the critters, I thank you.

As I said, Weggie and I thank you for your years of care and concern. Please don't tell the new guy about Weggie. I'd like him to start with a clean slate, if you know what I mean. Neither of us takes rejection very well.

CATTITUDE

*Cat's pajamas: What a cat should wear
at the vet clinic if he's staying overnight.*

THE CAT RULES

As They Apply to the Vet's

RULE 1
The cat must go to the vet's for monthly … okay, occasional …
okay, annual checkups. Okay, emergencies are mandatory.

RULE 2
No way I'm going to the vet's. I've developed
a holistic approach to good health.

RULE 3
I know it's noisy at the vet's,
but we can't afford private health care.

RULE 4
Best behaviour? If I do as I please at home,
what makes you think I'll behave at the vet's?

RULE 5
I will not stay overnight at the vet's. Have you heard the screams in
the cage room? It's like an Abu Ghraib prison for pets back there.

RULE 6
That dog was old and minding his own business.
You had no right to whack him. Now it's on your record.

RULE 7
Oh yeah? If the vet did that to a kid, he'd be charged.

RULE 8
Cats have a separate oral pouch where pills
are stored so we can spit them out an hour later.

RULE 9
How about a collar that electronically flashes my body
temperature and we get rid of that thermometer thing?

RULE 10
So the vet takes all the embarrassing stuff that happens
to us and blabs it to some guy writing a book?
Whatever happened to cat–client confidentiality?

26

Father's Day—My Son Is a Freakin' Furball

Cats know how to obtain food without labour,
shelter without confinement, and love without penalties.

W. L. GEORGE

I was quite taken by Barbara Diamond's column in *Cat Fancy* magazine when she wrote: "Men who love cats are a special breed, so this month, when fathers of every size, shape, and persuasion are honoured, I would like to propose a tribute to the men who are parents of cats."

I never thought of myself as a pet parent—only the disgruntled owner of one.

Coincidentally, I find that baby-talk stuff—"Oh, look! Muffy left Mommy a widdle pwesent!"—a bunch of crap.

I cringe when I hear a woman call her dog by saying, "There's a good boy. Come to Mommy." I want to say to her, "Lady, your husband has to be the ugliest man on earth."

However, last week I received in the mail a Father's Day card that was signed, "With love, your son, Weggie."

Forgive my suspicions about such a touching gesture, but Weggie can't write. If he could, I'm sure I'd be constantly painting over a lot of cat graffiti, like, "Keep cats happy. Neuter more dogs."

And certainly, Weggie has not figured out how the postal system works. If he has, I think he has an obligation to tell me so I can pass the information along to Canada Post.

And "love"? Me? Weggie loves plump rodents, summer snoozes in the cool of my office window, chasing rubber balls, drinking from dripping taps, and hiding behind drapes to scare the hell out of me. But love me? Love the gentle and nurturing *Cat Fancy* parent, expressive of feelings and self-confident enough not to be threatened by my cat's inscrutable nature? I don't think so.

Unfortunately, I'm little more than Weggie's personal valet and appointments secretary. Our relationship is strictly business. I open the door and tins of food according to his daily schedule, and drive him back and forth to the vet's when he needs medical attention, and in return … and in return … Okay, our business relationship is a one-way street.

Essentially, I coddle and protect him—giving him the best food, toys, and medical care a writer's income will allow—and he rewards me by keeping me awake half the night worrying about what he's up to.

Anyway, there's no doubt in my mind that if I vanished tomorrow, that little rake would replace me with a temp, which naturally my estate would pay for.

"Hello, Temp Services? My regular guy just croaked, and I was wondering what you have available in your Blue Blood Royalty Treatment Program?"

No, I really don't like that cutesy-wutesy stuff between people and their pets. And to look upon Weggie as some sort of teenage son struggling through his adolescent years is too ridiculous to even contemplate.

About the only thing Weggie has in common with a teenage kid is that he goes to his room and sulks for a couple of hours after I scold him for doing something wrong.

That, and he wouldn't know how to operate a coat hanger or pick up after himself if his very life depended on it. I mean, if I ever actually witnessed Weggie putting his things away or helping with the dishes, I'd probably die right there on the spot.

So, sure, there are a few similarities, small coincidences really, between my cat and a teenage kid. He's continually sassing me back, but this may just be a rebellious stage he's going through. Oh, he's got an attitude, all right, and some days I think that chip on his shoulder could only be removed by surgery.

And well, yes, as a matter of fact, he does, once in a while, stay out half the night. And when he does get in the house, he looks like something a kid ... sorry, a cat dragged in. And I'm awake all night, checking the patio door every half hour to see if he's come home.

Every time I reprimand him, he gives me that "Gee whiz" look, as if to say, "All the other cats get to stay out half the night, Bill."

However, I've never smelled alcohol on his breath or caught him with condoms, so for the time being, I'll take him at his word.

So that's where the pet/son comparison ends, except that I know he's experimented with drugs—namely, uncut catnip–and I gave him a stern lecture about it, but the only response I got was a silly grin and a somersault in his cardboard box. I probably should have waited until the next day, when he was straight.

Lately, he has been kind of aloof, but I suppose he's just establishing his own identity, becoming his own "person," so to speak. I know he needs his space, but it's kind of hard for me to come to grips with the fact that he's pursuing personal goals that don't necessarily include me.

Watching Weggie these days, I remember myself as a teenager—acting cool, staying out late, chasing the chicks, and jumping on unsuspecting field mice and biting their little heads off. Yeah, I led a pretty wild life back then.

So the silly notion that I'm somehow the single parent of a pet son named Weggie is just so preposterous ... Well, here. Have a look at the picture I carry of him in my wallet. See? We don't even look alike, for goodness' sake. (Did you ever see a cuter birthmark than that little dot on his nose, right there?)

No, I'm sorry, but animals are uncivilized creatures and people are ... Oh, here he comes now, off the neighbour's porch, up my fence, over the windowsill of my office—and what's that in his mouth? It's still twitching. Isn't that special? A gift. Hey! That's my boy!

"Come here, Weggie. Let's see if we can still save the little chipmunk. Come to Poppa. No, I mean it, come to Daddy. Now! You drop him this instant or you're grounded!"

Okay, to single fathers of cats everywhere—a heartfelt hug and a reciprocal purr on your special Feline Father's Day. There, I said it. Now can we please move on? I love him to death but frankly with this father and son thing, my cat is creeping me out.

CATTITUDE

Cat's meow: All of the above, with audio.

THE CAT RULES

As They Apply to the Father/Cat Thing

RULE 1
I demand a paternity test. Okay, then,
we both demand a paternity test.

RULE 2
If you tell any of the other cats about the "Daddy"
thing, I'll have you neutered again.

RULE 3
No, there is no father/son banquet, okay?

RULE 4
Please. You don't even *like* camping.

RULE 5
Quality time? You spend more time
with rodents than you do with me!

RULE 6
No, you still have a birth father—God, the lies
I must tell—and I'm sure he loves you very much.

RULE 7
Yes, your birth mother did have a number of litters
by different toms, but please don't call her that.

RULE 8
I hate the word "orphan." Let's go with "stepson."

RULE 9
No, I love you, but I will not drool on you to prove it.

RULE 10
Of course pets go to heaven. Weggie, see ya there.

Pets—they make us crazy,
and they make us better people.

THE CAT DICTIONARY

As a pet, a dog is your buddy, and he communicates with you.
A cat is your buddy, too, but he just doesn't speak your language.

PETER BORCHELT, AUTHOR

For a pet that does not speak, or even bark, the cat has produced a remarkable body of words. Here, then, are but a few:

Catabolism ...
> The high rate at which you burn calories trying to keep tabs on your cat.

Cataclysm ...
> The violent upheaval felt around the house on the day the cat arrives.

Catlick ...
> Like a cowlick, but cuter.

Catalectic ...
> What happens if your cat persists in playing with the wall socket.

Catalogue ...
> A record the cat keeps to prove he never did any of those things.

Catatonic ...

> A refreshing feline summer spritzer. Add gin at your own risk.

Catalyst ...

> A tipsy feline, leaning hard to one side after too many catatonics.

Catamaran ...

> A double-hulled sailing ship used by the sixteenth-century felines that discovered Catalina Island.

Catamite ...

> The explosive power used to throw a hairball halfway across a room.

Catamountain ...

> A feline theme park in Catavalley, California.

Catapult ...

> A hamstring injury caused by leaping at birds.

Cataract ...

> A professional performing arts class for cats that go on to do Disney films or pet food commercials.

Catastrophe ...

> Every cat's middle name.

Catbird ...
>   An accidental crossbreeding experiment that produced a flying feline that poops only on statues of dogs.

Catcall ...
>   Begins with "Yo!" and is often heard near construction sites.

Catcant ...
>   A language peculiar to one species of animal—namely, the chatty and almost always pissed-off feline.

Catchy ...
>   Tai chi for felines.

Catechu ...
>   Gesundheit.

Category ...
>   The crime scene on your patio.

Cater ...
>   To serve a cat hand and foot. Get used to it.

Catfish ...
>   Cathunt. Cat not come home for supper.

Cat flap ...
> A dog door used by the cat.

Catgut ...
> Garfield at his heaviest.

Cathedral ...
> A place of worship, where the cat sits and you kneel.

Catheter ...
> Don't even go there.

Catholic ...
> A feline that's addicted to communion wine.

Catacomb ...
> The last grooming procedure after the catlick.

Catnip ...
> The feline drug of choice.

Cat's cradle ...
> A feline tribute to the memory of Harry Chapin.

Cat's-tail ...
> Chased but seldom caught.

Catsup ...

> The cute, non-subtle way cats have of letting you know they're awake, and you should be too (often a nudge to the nose with a paw, as in, "I'm up").

Catty ...

> A conversation in which female claws are exposed, but there's not a cat in sight.

Clowder ...

> A cluster of cats, and a dog's worst nightmare.

Curiosity killed the cat ...

> And satisfaction brought it back.

Caterwaul ...

> The round heard after someone remarks, "Let's put them in the same room. I'm sure they'll get along."

Not enough room to swing a cat ...

> Actually refers not to the cat but to the cat-o'-nine-tails, once used on sailors below deck.

Cataplexy ...

> The complete bewilderment of a person who cannot understand how he ever wound up with a cat, or what he'll ever do without him.

ACKNOWLEDGMENTS

First and foremost, I thank the folks at Penguin Canada. From my editor, Barbara Berson, to my publicist, Lia Lyons, with Shima Aoki in between, you are the nicest, most efficient group of publishing people with whom I have ever worked. Even the receptionist, Maria Coletta McLean, is a treat to deal with.

Thanks go as well to my agent, Daphne Hart, and my freelance editor, Janice Weaver. Thank you, George Duma, my newspaper editor, who is both a friend and a pain in the ass.

Great gratitude goes to my assistant, Cathy Pelletier, who, with what she thinks are small suggestions and additions, makes me a better writer.

To the Different Drummer's Richard Bachman and other great independent bookstore operators, thank you for promoting and selling my books.

To Don and Lisa Graham at Crew's Quarters in Port Colborne, Ontario, thank you for supporting me, my books, and my author series, Readings at the Roselawn.

And to all the noble and struggling organizations like Welland's Kitty Cat Keep, thank you and do not stop welcoming the unwanted. Thank you to Sandie Morrison for giving "Dustin" a second life.

Erin the bartender—you're the best! (Why does it always come down to a bartender?)